WEST

COAST

WAVE

WEST COAST WAVE

NEW CALIFORNIA HOUSES

DIRK SUTRO

VAN NOSTRAND REINHOLD
NEW YORK

Library of Congress Catalog Card Number 93-20856
ISBN 0-442-00957-7

I(T)P Van Nostrand Reinhold is an International Thomson Publishing company.
ITP logo is a trademark under license.

Printed in Hong Kong

Van Nostrand Reinhold   International Thomson Publishing GmbH
115 Fifth Avenue   Konigswinterer Str. 518
New York, NY 10003   5300 Bonn 3
                                         Germany

International Thomson Publishing   International Thomson Publishing Asia
Berkshire House,168-173   38 Kim Tian Rd., #0105
High Holborn, London WC1V 7AA   Kim Tian Plaza
England   Singapore 0316

Thomas Nelson Australia   International Thomson Publishing Japan
102 Dodds Street   Kyowa Building, 3F
South Melbourne 3205   2-2-1 Hirakawacho
Victoria, Australia   Chiyada-Ku, Tokyo 102
                                         Japan

Nelson Canada
1120 Birchmount Road
Scarborough, Ontario
M1K 5G4, Canada

16 15 14 13 12 11 10 9 8 7 6 5 4 3 2 1

Library of Congress Cataloging-in-Publication Data

Sutro, Dirk.
    West Coast wave : new California houses / Dirk Sutro.
        p.   cm.
    Includes index.
    ISBN 0-442-00957-7
    1. Architecture, Postmodern—California. 2. Deconstructivism
(Architecture)—California. 3. Architect-designed houses—
California. I. Title.
NA7235.C2S88   1993
728'.37'0922794—dc20   93-20856
                                                  CIP

CONTENTS

FOREWORD
BY DAVID GEBHARD

If one has had the opportunity of perusing the architectural journals and the upper middle-class shelter magazines over the past few years, it is obvious that California's contingent of "modernist" architects has obtained a high degree of national recognition and well-deserved respect. Even the popular news magazines have, over the past few years, presented numerous articles and illustrations of the work of Frank O. Gehry and of many of his younger colleagues from Southern California and the Bay Region of San Francisco.

California, of course, has had a long history of influencing architectural design, taste, and fashion throughout the country and abroad. First, just after the turn of the century, there was the Mission Revival and the California Bungalow, then the national rage in the mid-1920s for the Spanish Colonial Revival, and finally in the 1930s and the post–World War II years, the California Ranch house. These tended to be popular exportations directed toward a middle-class audience and only incidentally for the country's aesthetic and architectural elite. But these waves of influence from California differ in a number of ways from the present inundation from Lotusland.

To a degree, the American public responds to the buildings of California's current "experimental modernists" somewhat the same as it reacted in the 1920s and early 1930s to Programmatic buildings in the form of Egyptian Sphinxes, to sell real estate, and enlarged Alice in Wonderland oranges, to sell orange juice. In the 1950s and early 1960s Americans responded to the uncontrolled riotousness of Googie restaurants. For the American public, these earlier California structures, and now the newest ones, seem to cater to our urge to be pulled from our normal world into a world of the unfamiliar.

For the current architectural elite, who are generally ponderously serious these days, the buildings being designed by California's new avant-garde contingent easily match in international significance John Entenza's famed Case Study Houses sponsored by *Arts and Architecture* magazine, which were produced from the late 1940s on into the early 1960s.

To understand the underlying approach reflected in the Case Study Houses and the buildings currently being produced by Frank O. Gehry, Eric Moss, Mark Mack, and others, one has to go back to the architectural world of the late nineteenth century. Although practicing architects had always, to one degree or another, thought of themselves as designers, they didn't become intensely self-conscious as artists until the nineteenth century.

It was in the mid to late nineteenth century (particularly in England) that those who were designing buildings began to refer to themselves as "Art-Architects."[1] This self-consciousness was fundamentally involved with aesthetic issues and was, of course, part of the Oscar Wilde adage "Art for Art's Sake." Certainly such nineteenth-century English architects as William Butterfield and William Burges viewed themselves in this manner. Out of the "Art for Art's Sake" movement emerged the personage of the architect as a cultural hero. As hero, the art-architect could estab-

---

[1] Alf Boe, *From Gothic Revival to Functional Forms.* (Oxford: Basil Blackwell, 1977) pp. 128–146.

lish in an ex cathedra manner what should or should not be considered as architecture.

The architect as the divine form giver underlies the approach to design of such turn of the century figures as Louis H. Sullivan, Frank Lloyd Wright, and Edwin Lutyens.[2] With the emergence of Post Modernism in the mid 1960s, the view of the architect as an art-architect was espoused by Robert Venturi, both in his buildings and in his many writings. California's contemporary avant-garde designers, as one would expect, think of themselves in this light, i.e., they think of themselves as artists creating art objects, in these cases, buildings.

While these present-day California architects fit comfortably into the world of "Art for Art's Sake," they differ radically from most practitioners of the past and even with many of their contemporaries. The architects of the Case Study Houses, Raphael S. Soriano, Craig Ellwood, Pierre Koenig, and the major American figures of Post Modernism, Robert Venturi and Charles Moore, thought and designed their structures within the traditional lineage of architecture. They were (and are) architects who are artists, whereas some of California's avant-garde practitioners are artists (sculptors) who use the media of buildings to design art objects. In some instances their buildings are essentially enlarged pieces of (or fragments of) sculpture. And if some of their structures were reduced in size and placed within the white walls of an art gallery, one could easily respond to them as effective pieces of pure sculpture.

Thus, although Venturi and Moore continue to look back to various historic architectural traditions, California's avant-garde has, in a number of instances, gone outside the traditional world of architecture and looked to the early modern art world of Post-Cubism, Dadism, Expressionism, Surrealism, and Constructionalism. Anyone familiar with the avant-garde art world of the twenties will easily discover the sources for some of the visual language which is now being employed by a number of California's present-day modernists in the sculptures of the German surrealist Kurt Schwitters or in the fantastic sets for the famed 1920's film *The Cabinet of Doctor Caligari.*

It is fascinating to note the very different reaction of the early modernist architects to avant-garde art of the teens and twenties, compared to the responses of many contemporary Californians. The early modernists sought inspiration from the art of the Cubists and Post Cubists, and they then transformed it into the traditional world of architecture. As a case in point, Le Corbusier maneuvered the Cubist image in his Purist paintings into the illusion of three-dimensional forms, and then proceeded to the next step of shifting these images into realizable architecture.

Going back further in time, the mid-nineteenth-century English architect William Butterfield, with his fondness for bold, "ugly," and nontraditional detailing and color, is often cited as a precursor of Post Modernism and even of Deconstructivism.[3] But a look into his approach to design illustrates that he held views of architecture decidedly different from many of today's avant-garde. "Distortion and disorder," he wrote, "for supposed good ends must have no permanent part in a building erected for [public worship] and which is to last for generations."[4] How different from this view is that of Eric Moss, who recently wrote that "the task of architecture is both to put things together and, simultaneously, to re-examine, to take things apart."[5] Equally indicative of a somewhat different approach to design is the comment of the leading figure of Post Modernism, Robert Venturi. His position was essentially similar to Butterfield's when he commented, in 1990, that "Disharmony that comes from circumstances that are valid has beauty."[6]

---

[2] The relationship between Post Modernism and Lutyens is explored in an article by Robert Venturi and Denise Scott Brown, "Learning from Lutyens," *Journal of the Royal Institute of British Architects* (August 1969): 353–354.

[3] For a discussion of the architectural intent of Butterfield see John Summerson, *Heavenly Mansions.* (London: The Cresset Press, 1949) pp. 159–176.

[4] William Butterfield, quoted in Paul Thompson, *William Butterfield: Victorian Architect.* (Cambridge: MIT Press, 1971) p. 33.

[5] Eric Moss, quoted in Herbert Muschamp, "An Enterprize Zone of the Imagination," *The New York Times* (March 14, 1993): Sec. H., p. 32.

[6] Kurt Anderson, "Robert Venturi and Denise Scott Brown Speak Out on Issues of Urban Contexturalism, Postmodernism and 'Disharmony'," *Architectural Design* (February 1990): p. 82.

In the realm of the aesthetic, does this California avant-garde group bespeak something which is regional to the place? The answer, as one would expect, is both yes and no. If one's view of California, and especially the Southland, is as a place which cultivates the non-familiar, then the answer is that many of these new buildings would easily qualify. But it would immediately have to be pointed out that the "Deconstructivist" tinge apparent in some of this California work is a design quality shared worldwide. It is certainly not something entirely unique to California. Perhaps it might be argued that there is an ad hoc quality about much of the California work not present elsewhere. But this quality is again shared by other contemporary designers practicing in Paris or Tokyo.

Critics have noted that a good number of earlier California avant-garde architects were building upon an already established "tradition" present in California. As a case in point, comparisons have been made between several designs (from the 1920s on through the late 1940s) of R.M. Schindler and current avant-garde work. At first glance, such projects as Schindler's Physical Education Lodge in Topanga Canyon (1923) and above all his 1949 Ellen Janson house in Hollywood might be mentioned as precursors; but a close look at these buildings illustrates that Schindler's intent comes closest to that of William Butterfield, rather than that of most of California's avant-garde architects. As far as architectural intent is concerned, Schindler was not essentially interested in making a statement and then taking it apart, as is certainly true of some current California designers.

Since the interest in and intent of this group of California architects is more often than not the aesthetic nature of the artifact they have created, it should not be surprising that they exhibit varying degrees of concern for the specificity of their surroundings, ranging from the environmental approach of Stanley Saitowitz in the Bay Area and Ted Smith's contextualism in San Diego, to the more objectified work of Frank Israel in Los Angeles and Randy Dalrymple in San Diego. In California, and especially in southern Calironia, the manipulation of the landscape (both ecologically and aesthetically) has often been as important as and at time as even more significant than the buildings. It could be suggested that perhaps some California avant-garde modernists feel uncomfortable dealing with the landscape because such a concern would force them to go outside the traditional walls of the museum.

If one grants their intent, however, then there is no question that this new group of California architects has created, and is creating, an impressive array of designs. The national and international admiration of and interest in their work is due to the high quality of their designs, together with the fact that they closely reflect many of the latest worldwide design approaches found in avant-garde circles. The designs of these California architects end up both reflecting the perceived atmosphere of California and at the same time sharing a number of concepts with the contemporary world at large.

University of California
Santa Barbara

PREFACE

West Coast Wave grew out of the idea that California is a special place that inspires special houses. The idea was to show several innovative new houses designed by California architects in or near the state's three largest cities, to give some idea how these houses grew out of their places, and to explore how they relate to, and/or depart from, the great Modern designs of the past.

"Modern" means many things to many people, and can refer to a range of styles and dogmas. The first definition given by the dictionary is "Of or pertaining to the present or recent time; not ancient." In that sense, all of these houses are Modern. They may not look at all alike, but they are sensitive reflections of their times and places.

Retrospective essays give an overview of important earlier architects and houses. Many architects and buildings were omitted for the sake of brevity, but I hope the book presents a meaningful cross section of the great houses, past and present, that place California on the cutting edge of residential design.

Dirk Sutro

ACKNOWLEDGMENTS

Thanks to David Gebhard and Sally Woodbridge, architectural historians and authors who made numerous useful suggestions. In the Bay Area, vital sources of information included Joe Esherick, Ken Cardwell, Vernon DeMars, Enrique Liamosner, Ann Bertelsen, and Richard Bender. Theresa Heyman and Drew Johnson at the Oakland Museum helped assemble photos by Roger Sturtevant. Robert Sweeney, Randall Makinson, Rick Gooding, Ray Kappe, Michael Rotondi, and Eric Moss gave vital input in Los Angeles. Pam Post sorted through R. M. Schindler's papers at U.C. Santa Barbara to find a few original, insightful comments. Jane Booth, Bruce Kamerling, and Tom Adama at the San Diego Historical Society provided information and helped locate historic photos. Also in San Diego, Phyllis Van Doren, Barbara Carlton, Kathleen Stoughton, and *San Diego Home/Garden* magazine contributed essential facts. Thanks to owners of great houses from the past who opened their doors for personal tours, and much appreciation to the gifted photographers whose work is included. Special thanks to my family for support, and to Bill W. and H.P. for guidance.

Orco Block, a leading manufacturer of concrete block in southern California, made a generous contribution toward photo costs. Thank you, Buck Johns and Pete Muth.

WEST

COAST

WAVE

SAN FRANCISCO

RETROSPECTIVE

BAY

BAY AREA

A big signature Maybeck fireplace warms the living room at the Chick house, where several glass doors make a strong connection to the outdoors. Richard Barnes

O n one of those overcast Berkeley Sundays when newspapers lie in driveways until mid-morning and the misty hills are serene, I follow Chabot Road east off College Avenue. For a mile or more, the scenery is as I remember it. The road is quaint and narrow and rises gradually as it threads back into the hills among houses. Some are Craftsman-era bungalows, others are clones of earlier East Coast and European styles.

A few more blocks and the placid spell of a quiet Sunday drive is broken. Cool jazz on the car radio is suddenly in harsh counterpoint to what's outside: the charred remains of the Oakland-Berkeley hills holocaust of 1991. I am looking for a particular special house, but find it difficult to believe that any still stand. What was once an old neighborhood aging gracefully beneath a canopy of coast live oaks and other mature trees is now a gutted, desolate landscape of twisted tree trunks, barren concrete pads, and broken pipes writhing in agony.

Maybe I've missed my destination. I head back down the hill and all at once I see it, miraculously spared amid the ruins. Although once-dense vegetation has evaporated and nearby houses are mere cinders, the home that Bernard Maybeck designed for Guy Chick still looks much as it did when completed in 1914.

Protected by an armor of redwood shingles and siding, the two-story structure rests solidly on its exposed concrete base, sheltered by the deep eaves of a redwood-beamed roof. It's a basic box of a house, but ingeniously modulated with subtle touches: the quatrefoil pattern used in wooden gates and railings, deep, inviting recesses for entries, Gothic arches, and a pocket second-story balcony that juts out, shaded by its own little roof, to announce the main entry. Foster Goldstrom, a New York art dealer, owns the place. He's a Maybeck devotee. The California plates on his Mercedes even say "Maybeck." He takes good care of the house and has already restored minor fire damage.

Maybeck's Chick house (1914) shows Swiss chalet influences in its materials and roof forms, and has eclectic detailing such as a Tudor arch over the kitchen entrance. Richard Barnes

Goldstrom invites me in and shows off a collection of weird contemporary art pieces he changes constantly. The pieces look right at home inside Maybeck's masterpiece. The house feels more contemporary than most "contemporary" homes. The floorplan is open and casual. Rooms are large and comfortable and flow easily from one to another, connected by hardwood floors. The living room has one of those giant concrete signature Maybeck fireplaces, framed by tall French doors. Generous panes of glass all around worship the gnarled oaks outside, blurring the distinction between indoor and outdoor spaces, providing plenty of natural light.

T ies that link the current crop of San Francisco Bay Area architects to Maybeck and other Modern Bay Area predecessors are not obvious. Yet consistent threads run through the area's architectural history, from Maybeck and peers, including Ernest Coxhead, Willis Polk, and Julia Morgan down through William Wurster, Gardner Dailey, Mario Corbett,

Joe Esherick, Charles Moore, and top architects practicing today. But these common threads through the last 100 years of Bay Area architecture have little to do with the common image of the Bay Area Tradition as rustic shingle-and-redwood cottages. Instead, Bay Area architects in the Modern era have shared a spirit, a way of responding to the region that operates on a deep, almost instinctual level, influencing siting, choice of materials, and ways of responding to climate and landscape.

Some current architects practicing in the Bay Area don't like the word *regionalism,* but they can't deny the area's magnetism and its influence on their work. Twentieth-century architects in the Bay Area have been seduced by the area's cultural, geographical, and historical matrix, forces that have inspired some of the West's most original architecture.

San Francisco has been a busy, sometimes bawdy, urban, nighttime town ever since gold seekers, empire builders, and entrepreneurs flocked to California during the mid-1800s. Mark Twain drank there, men like Mark Hopkins, Leland Stanford, and Charles Crocker gentrified Nob Hill with mansions to go with their dynasties. Carol Doda's bust was the best-known cultural attraction in North Beach for years. The Beat generation spouted poetry and jazz during the fifties, sixties hippies made this the capital of peace, love, and acid rock, and the Gay movement has found an accommodating headquarters in San Francisco in contemporary times. Frank Sinatra once summed the place up as "a grown-up, swinging town."

Across the Bay, the Oakland/Berkeley axis, with the University of California as its cultural hub, is a Bay Area focus for intellectual and academic life. Berkeley is a genuine university town where coffeehouses serve up mudlike espresso to bleary eyed students who hang out until the wee hours, carrying on the rebellious, discursive spirit of the sixties.

Despite the area's colorful history and cultural traditions, Bay Area architecture through most of the twentieth century has relied more on depth and subtlety than the colorful, showy architectural displays that get the most attention in Los Angeles. Today's Bay architects are taking risks, but the best of them value problem-solving and deeper, enduring qualities over appearances. Architects such as Mark Mack, Stanley Saitowitz, Daniel Solomon, and Fernau and Hartman care as much about what their houses feel like inside as they do about what they look like. The outsides of their houses can take radical forms, but in most cases these are generated by practical concerns such as daylighting, structural integrity, view orientation, and the flow of interior spaces.

Houses included in this book respond thoughtfully to their larger regional settings and more intimate contexts, but not in the same ways as their predecessors. Wave forms inspired the sassy kick of the roof on a beach house designed by Saitowitz. Ace Architects drew on Bay Area traditions of fantasy and eclectic international borrowing to come up with a Turkish fantasy house in Berkeley. Richard Stacy of Tanner Leddy Maytum Stacy extends Bay Area customs of using basic, utilitarian materials with Craftsman-era care, and giving meticulous attention to the intricate play of light and space within deceptively simple-looking shells. The artists' loft designed by Stacy and included in this book uses a machine-age Modern aesthetic not common to the Bay Area, but the place is perfectly suited to its San Francisco warehouse district. Architects David Baker and Nancy Whitcombe used Maybeck's work as a point of departure for a house they call "Revenge of the Stuccoids," a physical and theoretical collision between the old and the new.

B ay Area houses are set in a region whose mythic qualities have exerted an essential influence on the shapes of local buildings. San Francisco has its rolling hills, steep streets, narrow lots, and frequent shrouds of fog, together with panoramic views of the Bay and such venerable local landmarks as Alcatraz, the Golden Gate, and Mt. Tamalpais. The Oakland-Berkeley hills, with their gentle stands of old eucalyptus and redwoods, have a pastoral, mystical beauty only enhanced at the moment by the barren, lunar landscapes left in the wake of the devastating 1991 fire, which wiped out some 3000 houses, including important houses by architects such as Moore, Maybeck, Morgan, Wurster, and Coxhead.

Other Bay Area locales have their own identities, but many of the best new houses in these areas also extend Bay region traditions. Fernau and Hartman's wine country house near Sonoma to the north, for example, continues the thoughtful space planning, inventive use of plain materials, sensitive siting, and straightforward exterior expression the architects admire in the work of predecessors such as Maybeck and Esherick. Down the peninsula south of San Francisco, in Hillsborough, a new place designed by House + House capitalizes on the Bay Area's longtime love affair with Mediterranean culture and design.

How, exactly, have settings inspired Bay Area architects?

One commonly noted quality of many Bay Area houses is their vertical orientation. In the past, this has sometimes been attributed to a desire to make a clean break with the horizontal Modern approach of the thirties through fifties. But the vertical volumes employed by architects ranging from Maybeck to Wurster and, today, Daniel Solomon and Jeremy Kotas have as much to do with steep sites as with a desire for formal innovation.

San Francisco's rolling hills and density have generated the stepped-up row house. Narrow sites forced the best architects to find creative solutions to problems of bringing in natural light, providing compact private outdoor spaces such as patios, gardens, or courtyards, and grabbing views through ingenious variations on the perennial projecting bay window. Architects built up rather than out to gain a sense of spaciousness. Since many of these urban dwellings are hard against their neighbors, with no possibility of side windows, their designers devised means of bringing natural light down from skylights and in through front and rear windows, through free-flowing interiors.

In the Oakland-Berkeley hills, lots can be as steep as San Francisco's. Some of these homes step up to hug their hillsides, others perch precariously on stilts of steel or wood or cantilever out daringly. The lack of confinement in these less-dense neighborhoods allows a more sculptural,

three-dimensional approach to the overall design of a house. No two sites are alike, but many have fantastic bay views. Rooms can be arranged to maximize views in several directions; this practical approach often produces more dynamic exteriors than can be found on narrow San Francisco lots that leave only the front facade as a canvas for innovation or a location for view-catching glass.

Early Bay Area homes by Maybeck and others utilized redwood, Douglas fir, local stone, and other indigenous materials that seemed to inspire extra care in their designers. While environmental concerns and innovations in materials are changing the Bay architect's palette, many of the best young architects, including Stacy, Kotas, David Baker and Nancy Whitcombe, and Fernau and Hartman, are also materials-conscious, using traditional stucco and wood in fresh, often sculptural ways, searching for unusual, sometimes utilitarian materials they can elevate to beautiful residential use through creative design.

Bay Area architects are producing their share of interesting work, but their architecture doesn't get as much coverage as some of the new architecture in Los Angeles. Perhaps that is because some of these young architects place the focus on design more than on public relations, a tradition that dates back to Maybeck and Esherick, who never had much interest in gaining major media exposure.

As renowned architectural critic Lewis Mumford noted in a 1949 essay on Bay Area architecture that appeared in a catalog for a show at the San Francisco Museum of Art, the region's architecture has never received the national or international exposure it deserves.

". . . perhaps the architects of the Bay Region are themselves partly to blame for this neglect: but for Bernard Maybeck's fine reticence, his work would have been hailed long ago as the West Coast counterpart to Wright's prairie architecture. Yet the impulse to bury their lights under a bushel, so foreign to our usual American tendency to over-expose, over-publicize, over-claim, was a highly honorable one: that example of humility and self-respect makes the older architects of the Bay Region school worthy leaders of a new generation."

There are other old and important traditions that feed Bay Area architecture. Despite increased traffic, smog, noise, and neighborhood densities, life in the Bay Area in the late twentieth century brings with it certain values that have been passed down through many generations.

A strong feeling for nature, in this beautiful setting, is only natural. The Sierra Club, founded in 1892 in the Bay Area with John Muir as first president, has grown into a well-known environmental watchdog agency with headquarters in San Francisco and national membership numbering around 600,000. The Bay Area can be foggy, cool, and damp, and Bay dwellers tend more toward practical, comfortable clothes, often in earthy hues. Their houses are often dressed as they are. Their southern California counterparts, caressed by temperate weather, fascinated with both Hollywood and beach culture, tend more toward experimental, colorful threads. Like their makers, Los Angeles houses tend to look more like a rock star headed for a Hockney opening than a Sierra Club lifer.

The Bay Area has a reputation as a place for thinkers, where people take a serious interest in both traditional and alternative culture and arts. The University of California and surrounding community of coffeehouses, pubs, and student and faculty housing have provided an intellectual focus—especially for architecture—since the days when Bernard Maybeck taught at the school. Key architects such as William Wurster, Joe Esherick, and Charles Moore extended this academic tradition through their involvement as architecture department chairs and faculty members at U.C. Berkeley.

But even in this generally open-minded environment, Bay Area residents can be protective of neighborhood heritage when it comes to new architecture. During the 1980s, the San Francisco Planning Department, pressured by neighborhood groups and led by Planning Director Dean Macris, developed a reputation for the autocratic control it exerted over buildings, from downtown high-rises to row houses in San Francisco's hilly residential districts. Bay windows on new buildings in old neighborhoods pleased the planning department. Downtown, planners dictated a new generation of more modest high-rises with idiosyncratic stepped-back tops, no matter how bad these stubby, misshapen buildings made the city look. The situation got so bad before Macris stepped down with the arrival of new mayor Frank Jordan's administration in 1992 that architects spent more time trying to find ways to circumvent the planning department than they did considering a project's essential design challenges. Mack, for example, built a solid practice and international reputation in San Francisco during the 1980s. But by 1992, he had started shifting his practice to southern California, where he felt more free to explore a range of architectural ideas.

When it comes to architectural history, the Bay Area has some of the strongest traditions in the state. Late in the nineteenth century, while San Diego and Los Angeles were still searching for architectural identities and builders were putting up ornate Victorians and East Coast salt boxes that had nothing to do with the unique qualities of those regions, architects in the Bay Area were already exploring new modes of architectural expression. Because many of these architects were new to the area, also probably because the San Francisco Bay Area was geographically isolated from the rest of the nation, these architects felt free to experiment with forms and combinations of materials that, in retrospect, seem uniquely appropriate.

During the 1890s, Willis Polk advanced the Victorian aesthetic by stripping away the icing. He used odd bay windows that allowed his row houses to scoop in views, and composed his facades with imaginative manipulation of scale and forms. Also at the turn of the century in the Bay Area, A. C. Schweinfurth evolved a shingled Craftsman vernacular with an early modern sense of abstraction and wit, as in his Berkeley Unitarian church (1898).

Born in England, Ernest Coxhead arrived in San Francisco in 1890 and eventually engaged in some of the kinds of European historicist borrowings in which Maybeck later indulged, combining steep English cottage roofs with Mission Revival quatrefoils, spicing up Shingle-style houses with

Coxhead's Porter (1904, left) and Waybur (1902, right) houses are basic wood shingle structures decked out with classical pediments, pilasters, and a Palladian window. © *Morley Baer*

classical pilasters and pediments and arched Palladian windows. Coxhead also made good use of windows, wrapping corners with them or using broad expanses of small-paned windows to improve daylighting.

Coxhead's intelligence and quirky sense of humor marked him as much more than a revivalist mix-and-matcher. In Sally Woodbridge's book *Bay Area Houses,* historian David Gebhard notes how Coxhead, Polk, and Schweinfurth (a leading proponent of Mission Revival) brought together a variety of formal elements with odd juxtapositions of scale that made their buildings complex and difficult to comprehend at a glance.

Coxhead's 1904 Porter house in San Francisco has a simple, shingled front facade with symmetrically arranged windows and is subtly decorated by a pair of flat pilasters flanking central windows and a small pediment atop the highest central window. The adjacent Waybur house (1902) has a predominantly flat front facade, but Coxhead went wilder with expression, added a second-level false balcony with a railing that steps up to express a staircase inside, daylit by a Palladian window, and he also gave the house a classical pediment above the front door.

Architects such as Louis C. Mullgardt, W. R. Yelland, and John Hudson Thomas also made significant contributions during the turn-of-the-century years.

Mullgardt came to San Francisco from Missouri in 1905, after working in St. Louis and spending two years in England. He worked briefly for Polk and George Alexander Wright before going on his own, and was a Craftsman-style architect with a penchant for Mission Revival detailing such as rough adobelike stucco walls and large exposed roof timbers.

Yelland had traveled extensively through France, and buildings such as his 1928 Thornberg Village apartment complex in Berkeley, with its round tower and big arched openings, and his Goss house in Piedmont, with its wavy shingle roof, had a fantastic fairy-tale cottage charm that has inspired current architects such as Ace Architects, whose work is included in this book.

Thomas, a U.C. Berkeley graduate who had studied under Maybeck, experimented with styles ranging from Mission Revival (the 1911 Locke house) to English half-timbered to stone castle (the 1928 Hume house in Berkeley).

In planning and appearance, there was nothing obviously Modern about houses by Mullgardt, Yelland, and Thomas, but their mixing of forms and historic details foreshadowed some of Charles Moore's 1960s Bay Area designs and more recent houses by architects such as Daniel Solomon and Ace Architects.

Julia Morgan was another important Bay Area architect during the early twentieth century. She worked for Maybeck and attended the École des Beaux-Art in Paris before opening her own office in 1904. Morgan is best known as the architect for William Randolph Hearst's castle in San Simeon, down the California coast from San Francisco, but she designed several modest houses in the Bay Area.

Her use of raw, basic materials such as wood and shingles paralleled Maybeck's, and she pared wood, stucco, and brick exteriors to a minimal mode of expression that allowed them to recede into lush landscapes and nestle into hillside sites.

B ut every region seems to have its singular hero, and in the Bay Area, that titan is undoubtedly Maybeck, even though his work is still not given extensive treatment in most major texts on American architecture. Mumford first wrote about Maybeck in his 1931 book *The Brown Decades*, but books on Modern architecture generally fail to acknowledge Maybeck's contribution, an intelligent modern blending of the local redwood-and-shingle cottage vernacular and eclectic historic borrowings that pointed the way for generations to come.

Maybeck was born in New York City in 1862 and was exposed to design and art early. His father, Bernhardt, was an architectural wood-carver and furniture craftsman who encouraged the young Maybeck to paint and draw. As a teenager, Maybeck worked at Pottier and Stymus, which designed interior furnishings for Pullman railroad parlor cars.

While Maybeck was studying at the prestigious École des Beaux-Arts in Paris during the mid-1880s, the school's philosophy was changing from neoclassicism rooted in ancient Greece and Rome to more eclectic designs in tune with changing society and new building technologies including steel, notes Sally Woodbridge in her book *Bernard Maybeck, Visionary Architect*. During his time at the École, Maybeck toured several medieval churches, impressed with their mystical power. His instruction at the École taught him the primacy of a building's floorplan and spatial organization over its external appearance. According to Woodbridge, this was later apparent in houses by Maybeck that had asymmetrical exteriors due to the organization of interior plans and volumes.

In New York in 1886, Maybeck landed a job at a firm founded by fellow former Beaux-Arts students Thomas Hastings and John Carrere and stayed for three years, while the firm designed the Ponce de Leon and Alcazar Hotels in St. Augustine, Florida, both cast of concrete with fragmented coral and shells mixed in.

In 1889, Maybeck tried to open an office in Kansas City, but couldn't find work, and landed in the Bay Area the following year. He worked for Coxhead, then A. Page Brown, credited with inspiring the first generation of Bay Area architects who decided the Victorian Queen Anne style was no longer relevant for their region.

By the mid-1890s, several architects now seen as mainstays of early Bay Region ideas were practicing in San Francisco. As Maybeck's biographer Kenneth Cardwell notes, none of the twenty architects listed in an 1890 edition of *California Architect and Building News* were Bay Area natives. Distanced by thousands of miles from European-via-East Coast tradition, set into a new, beautiful region of moody but temperate weather, fantastic bay views, and thickly treed hills, such architects as Maybeck, Coxhead, Polk, and Schweinfurth began to design buildings that responded to the region through choice of materials, siting, and orientation to the outdoors.

Maybeck designed his first Bay Area house in 1895, for his friend Charles Keeler, author of *The Simple Home*, a book published in 1905 that expressed many of Maybeck's ideas about designing houses suited to California. It remains the definitive book from the period on West Coast Craftsman architecture.

Keeler's book (reissued in 1979 with an introduction by Dimitri Shipounoff) prescribed something much more than mere architectural style. It advocated a new outdoors-oriented lifestyle appropriate for a sunny, stimulating climate. Keeler and Maybeck helped organize the Hillside Club to protect precious hillsides and canyons in Berkeley, north of the U.C. campus, from development. Keeler knew John Muir and was an early member of the Sierra Club. In *The Simple Home*, Keeler urged the architects of the Bay region to develop honest, indigenous modes of expression inspired by the setting, to draw on native materials as much as possible.

To Keeler, ". . . hillside architecture is landscape gardening around a few rooms for use in case of rain." He called for gardens as extensions of interior living spaces.

In his deftly written, emotionally charged book, Keeler brought such heroes of his as Polk, Coxhead, and Maybeck together under a singular straightforward philsophy of design, focusing on Maybeck.

". . . his idea was to glorify the materials, not to hide them away, as if in shame under paint and plaster," Keeler wrote. "His ornament was found in structural emphasis. The timbers were exposed, the strength and character of the construction made the design."

Although the home as envisioned by Keeler would be simple, it would also be painstakingly crafted.

The San Francisco earthquake of 1906 prompted Maybeck to design the concrete Lawson house (1908). Bancroft Library

Maybeck's Goslinsky house (1909) in Berkeley showed the architect's shingled Craftsman aesthetic, but also his penchant for witty decoration, such as "eyebrows" that make the front facade resemble a human face. © Morley Baer

"We botch our carpentering and trust to putty, paint, and paper to cover up the defects," he wrote. "On Sundays we preach about the goodly apple rotten at the heart, and all the while we make houses of veneer and stucco . . . In the simple home all is quiet in effect, restrained in tone, yet natural and joyous in its frank use of unadorned material. Harmony of line and balance of proportion is not obscured by meaningless ornamentation; harmony of color is not marred by violent contrasts. Much of the construction shows, and therefore good workmanship is required and the craft of the carpenter is restored to its old-time dignity."

Maybeck designed several rustic shingle homes after Keeler's, the earliest of them in the same Berkeley neighborhood north of the University of California campus. After 1900, Maybeck went through a period of designing modified Swiss-chalet-style houses, with deep-eaved gable roofs and assorted decorative wood details inside and out, including the Flagg, Boke, Hopps, and Schneider houses, nestling many of these into hillsides with minimal grading.

Maybeck broadened his repertoire with the 1907 Lawson house, built of reinforced concrete after the 1906 San Francisco earthquake had devastated the city and geologist John Lawson, Maybeck's client, discovered that a major earthquake fault ran through his Berkeley property. Maybeck's explorations of concrete came during the same period as Irving Gill's in San Diego.

The Lawson house is a rectangular box, with simple but beautiful decoration including diamond patterns scored in exterior plaster, colored red and tan, and with tiny diamond tiles accentuating intersections of the scored lines. A sleeping porch pushes out from one side, with a half-round deck that cantilevers from the building, and there is a second sleeping porch on the other end of the house. The plan is simple, open, and symmetrical. On the first floor, for example, the central entry axis divides the kitchen and dining rooms on one side from living and billiard rooms on the other. As Woodbridge notes in her book on Maybeck, the architect elevated common materials to elegant decorative use, such as stairway balustrades of black plaster cast in a scroll motif.

In appearance, the Lawson house was as close as Maybeck came to the stripped-down, basic style of Gill, the San Diego architect who was designing

The Kennedy house mixes Tudor arched windows with a Mediterranean tile roof and colorful stucco walls. © Morley Baer

Maybeck's cottage (1924), known as "the studio," was built after an earlier home burned down in the 1923 Berkeley fire. The exterior was covered with experimental Bubblestone— burlap dipped in liquid cement, hung on wires. Bancroft Library

his first spare, cubistic Modernist houses around this time. Most of Maybeck's houses were quirky and eclectic in appearance, not minimal Modern, but they were often more Modern inside, with wide door openings and hallways marrying generously daylit rooms together, and with generous numbers of windows bringing in daylight and joining rooms to gardens. In the tradition of Frank Lloyd Wright, Maybeck believed in total design and often designed furniture, light fixtures, and elaborate concrete or plaster fireplace surrounds. He frequently added wood trefoil or quatrefoil details, one of his signatures, and many of his homes featured baronial living rooms with redwood walls, gigantic fireplaces, and soaring ceilings supported by heavy carved or gracefully tapered wood beams.

Maybeck's 1914 Kennedy studio is one of his classic eclectic houses, combining half-timbering, a medieval arch, a tile roof, and exterior railings cast of concrete in a quatrefoil pattern.

Some of Maybeck's later houses were progressive departures from his trademark abundant use of wood inside and out. In 1924, Maybeck designed a small Berkeley house for himself and his wife with exterior walls covered with Bubblestone, an experimental foamy liquid concrete material into which pieces of burlap were dipped then nailed to wall studs. The large house he designed for his son Wallen in Kensington, completed in 1937, has concrete walls, steep metal roofs, and steel-sash windows, a response to a fire-prone grassy setting.

Over the years, the handcrafted, earthy aesthetic that began with Maybeck and his peers was handed down through a line of leading Bay Area architects: Wurster, Esherick, and architects such as Fernau and Hartman today. This lineage is easily traceable. Laura Hartman moved to the Bay Area from West Virginia to go to architecture school at U.C. Berkeley because she admired Esherick and other Bay Area giants. Esherick knew Wurster and liked the simplicity of his work. Wurster often spoke of his love of materials.

In a 1964 interview conducted as part of U.C. Berkeley's Regional Cultural History Project, Wurster, who died in 1973, explained the strong connection he felt to Maybeck and spoke of "the cleanliness of the wood . . . how it is so fresh at the beginning and it smells so nice." In 1941, while showing architecture critic Lewis Mumford some Bay Area buildings, Wurster further elaborated, for Mumford, his debt to Maybeck.

A gigantic Maybeckian fireplace roared at the heart of his modest studio, with its intricately detailed woodwork. Bancroft Library

Wurster's Gregory farmhouse (1926–27) evokes simple rural farmhouses and is laid out around a central court. Roger Sturtevant Collection, Oakland Museum

"I learned from William Wurster's lips the direct effect of Maybeck's poetic architectural imagination on his own work, while still a student at Berkeley," Mumford wrote in his essay for the catalog for the 1949 "Domestic Architecture of the San Francisco Bay Region" exhibit at the San Francisco Museum of Art.

True to his words, Wurster's buildings are simple, but they are also, in their own way, radical, for example in the extreme ways that he integrated indoor and outdoor spaces.

Unlike most of the key twentieth-century Bay architects, Wurster was a native. He was born in Stockton in 1895 and earned his architecture degree from U.C. Berkeley in 1919. He later attended graduate school at Harvard in city planning, and from 1944 to 1950, was dean of Architecture at the Massachusetts Institute of Technology. He returned to the Bay Area as dean of Architecture at Berkeley from 1950 to 1959, and was dean of the College of Environmental Design from its inaugural year, 1959, until 1963.

Wurster was well acquainted with the leading Modern architects of his day, including Marcel Breuer and Mies van der Rohe, and he once confessed to an interviewer that he considered Alvar Aalto his god among architects. Wurster was also familiar with the work of southern California architects, and once lived in a Berkeley house designed by Los Angeles architect R. M. Schindler, one of the most innovative architects in the southern half of the state.

But Wurster transcended his reverence for Maybeck and his close personal ties to the Modernists with a unique, straightforward, personal style of his own. Between 1927 and 1942, he designed more than 200 houses, favoring simple, sometimes even crude construction. Structure, materials, and appearances weren't as important to him as the lives his houses nurtured, the views and close contact with the outdoors they encouraged, the fresh air and natural light they provided.

Early in his career, Wurster began a longtime association with landscape designer Thomas Church. Their collaborations strengthened the intimate ties between house and landscape advocated by Keeler and Maybeck. Obviously, Wurster subscribed to Modern ideas about open planning, abundant natural light, and new efficient lifestyles promoted by a new architecture. But by couching these ideas in a simple architectural language inspired by the Bay region, he created houses with a timeless, livable appeal few of the spare classic Modern houses of his time can claim.

Interior walls of the Gregory farmhouse are painted redwood, floors are unfinished redwood. Roger Sturtevant Collection, Oakland Museum

One of Wurster's inventions was the "kitchen cave," an indoor/outdoor dining space like this one at the Hollins house (1931) in Pasatiempo, in the Santa Cruz Mountains. Roger Sturtevant Collection, Oakland Museum

Wurster's Dondo house (1935) on San Francisco at Point Richmond is made of precast concrete block that stands up to saltwater weathering. Roger Sturtevant Collection, Oakland Museum

Although Wurster was the most important of a second generation of California architects who responded to the Bay region in fresh ways, and obviously extended certain traditions that began with Maybeck, Wurster felt it was dangerous to speak of a Bay Area Tradition. If it existed, he believed, it certainly had nothing to do with style.

"Style is a word—one time many years ago Lewis Mumford in a *Skyline* article said something about the Bay Region style by Maybeck and Wurster' and I wish he'd never used the word because it's a Bay Region characteristic of open-mindedness more than a style," Wurster said during his interview for U.C. Berkeley's Cultural History Project. "A style is something that's adopted by a number of not necessarily thinking people and pushed through to exhaustion . . . For many reasons style was the wrong word to use. It should have been Bay Region atmosphere or Bay Region tendencies or something like that, because actually the freedom of living out here without any flies, with no cold, no hot, means you have sort of an in- and out-of-door living that's possible nowhere else in this country."

The Gregory house (1926–27) near Santa Cruz, Wurster's best-known masterpiece, is a recapitulation of vernacular farmhouses and a long-standing California tradition of courtyard houses that dates back to the days of the Spanish ranchos. Rooms in the L-shaped house face out on a central courtyard. A covered outdoor corridor ties the rooms together and serves as a transitional space between the public courtyard and more private spaces within the house. Wurster used familiar farmhouse materials in this rural setting, including walls of inch-thick vertical redwood siding that support the roof without a conventional 2 X 4 frame. A water tower in front of the house may have been inspired by similar structures Wurster saw when he was growing up near Stockton. At any rate, it's a simple but emotionally charged icon: a reminder of the region's rural past and a beacon to visitors.

Wild young 1990s Bay Area architects? No. Wurster, using corrugated siding in 1940 on the Saxton-Pope house in Orinda. Roger Sturtevant Collection, Oakland Museum

Like other California Modernists, Wurster liked big openings that merge indoor and outdoor space, such as these huge sliding panels at the Clark house (1937) in Aptos. Roger Sturtevant Collection, Oakland Museum

Two of Wurster's trademark inventions were the "kitchen cave," a kitchen/dining room open on one or more sides to the outdoors, and the "room with no name," a large, centrally located flexible room that served as a transitional space between other, more private rooms.

The Butler house (1931–32) is formally laid out, with pavilions situated at the corners of a square plan, tied together by covered veranda/corridors. Living in the house involves continually moving between indoor and outdoor spaces, a free-flowing scheme of circulation designed for a Bay Area climate that is mild more than half of each year.

Several of Wurster's later houses still seem contemporary. The Saxton-Pope house in Orinda (1940) used concrete block and corrugated metal siding, readily available materials popular with some of the new generation of California architects. The Dondo residence (1935), on San Francisco Bay at Point Richmond, was built from another type of precast concrete block that would withstand harsh weathering in its bayfront setting. The Coleman house of 1962, designed by Wurster with longtime partners Theodore Bernardi and Donn Emmons (Wurster is actually not given much credit for its design) featured two-story interior glass walls that pull in natural light from a central courtyard.

Despite its many subtleties, Wurster's unpretentious approach was slow to gain the respect of

Wurster's Stevens house in San Francisco had an industrial aesthetic of concrete block, corrugated siding, and tall cylindrical smokestacks. Roger Sturtevant Collection, Oakland Museum

Wurster had little to do with Wurster, Bernardo & Emmons's design of the Coleman house (1962), which wraps dramatically around a central courtyard garden. Roger Sturtevant Collection, Oakland Museum

Easterners, a prejudice that continues today, since top design publications are all based on the East Coast.

"Historians like [Henry Russell] Hitchcock looked down on Wurster," says Enrique Limosner, a professor of architectural history at San Diego City College, who gives a three-hour lecture on Wurster. "Before his International Style book was published, he came out here looking for something great, but Wurster didn't fit that pattern. What they were doing out here was rather old shoe and unassuming. Mr. Wurster exemplified that, but that was an achievement. Most young architects want to flex their muscles and show off."

Wurster never felt compelled to flex his design muscles for the architectural establishment. While he probably isn't as well known outside the Bay Area now as he was in his prime, his work has been well appreciated by a handful of important historians.

"Few architects have produced work that is at once so innovative and so reassuring," notes Sir

Bannister Fletcher's massive *A History of Architecture*, the bible for undergraduate architecture students.

During the years immediately before and after World War II, a new generation of Bay Area architects added new, important work, including Gardner Dailey, John Funk, John Ekin Dinwiddie, Mario Corbett, Roger Lee, Joe Esherick, Vernon DeMars, and the partnership of Charles Warren Callister and Jack Hillmer, who shared a fascination with fine wood craftsmanship and Japanese design. Most of these architects were bound into the region by their associations with each other and their predecessors, and, in many cases, U.C. Berkeley. Esherick had worked for Dailey, a more style-conscious competitor of Wurster's. Wurster recruited Esherick to teach at Berkeley in 1952, and Esherick chaired the architecture school from 1977 to 1981. DeMars was a Wurster protege who taught at Berkeley from 1953 to 1975 and chaired the architecture department from 1959 to 1962. Charles Moore, who emerged as a leading Bay Area architect during the 1960s with his buildings at Sea Ranch, the northern California seaside community, and other Bay Area houses, had worked for Corbett and shared Corbett's fascination with plans that broke out of the rectilinear grid.

Funk, a U.C. Berkeley grad and former associate of Wurster, used meticulously detailed wood and built-in furniture in the Turner house (1938). Roger Sturtevant Collection, Oakland Museum

Dinwiddie, a Modernist mentored by Eliel Saarinen at the University of Michigan, tweaked the Modern box with the rigorously composed Roos residence (1939), adding a canted bay and pop-up chimney. Roger Sturtevant Collection, Oakland Museum

Born's own house (1951) in San Francisco was an uncompromising redwood box, with a high-ceilinged central living area connected to the garden by a wall of glass. Roger Sturtevant Collection, Oakland Museum

Floor-to-ceiling sliding doors opened the Roos residence wide to the garden. Roger Sturtevant Collection, Oakland Museum

Dinwiddie used variegated wood siding to help blend the Taylor residence (1941) with its woodsy setting in Ross, in Marin County. Roger Sturtevant Collection, Oakland Museum

Corbett's woodsy, sometimes organic-looking houses nestled into the natural terrain, like this place in Marin County (1948). Roger Sturtevant Collection, Oakland Museum

A winglike roof that touches down on the roof below and thin latticework that stripes the side of the house with thin shadows are among unconventional touches on Dailey's Le David residence. A contemporary of Wurster, Dailey had a more refined touch. Roger Sturtevant Collection, Oakland Museum

Lee used floor-to-ceiling glass to merge the Cedric Wright studio (1950s) in Lafayette with the outdoors. Colliding lines and forms create a disorienting effect more characteristic of 1990s designs. Roger Sturtevant Collection, Oakland Museum

Hill worked with Dinwiddie from 1938 to 1946 and later designed several houses on his own, including the Luchetti house (1960s), a light composition of brick, wood, and glass. Roger Sturtevant Collection, Oakland Museum

Esherick, who joined Mies van der Rohe, Le Corbusier, Eero Saarinen, and I. M. Pei as a recipient of the prestigious American Institute of Architects' gold medal, in 1988, is the obvious Bay region standard-bearer of his generation. He continues Wurster's no-frills attitude toward forms and materials, along with a respect for the wishes and needs of clients that began with Maybeck and Wurster.

Like other significant Bay architects, Esherick was initially an outsider. Born in Philadelphia in 1914, he earned his architecture degree from the University of Pennsylvania in 1937. Frank Lloyd Wright was one of his early heroes. The other was Le Corbusier. Esherick traveled in Europe after graduation, where he met Aalto by chance in a Stockholm library.

Esherick arrived in San Francisco in 1938, and his first architectural jobs were in the offices of Dailey and Walter Steilburg, an architect and engineer who had supervised construction on some of Julia Morgan's buildings. Esherick had already seen Wurster and Dailey's work in design journals.

"Gardner was always enormously concerned with how you lived in a building," Esherick recalls. "How the furniture was arranged, how you could have a feeling of repose and comfort and security, so that you could sit down in a chair and not feel you were going to have to pull your legs in every minute to get out of the way. He was concerned with things like how the dining room table was oriented to light that was pleasant for people on both sides."

Esherick worked for Dailey, but he had a greater affinity for Wurster.

"Wurster was less concerned with detail and more concerned in a sort of ideological way with a house as an expression of a new kind of egalitarian, servant-free living. I knew more people in Bill's office, and I was friendlier with him than Gardner in some ways."

Steilburg took Esherick to meet Maybeck in Berkeley. Years later, Maybeck advised Esherick during the design of the Pelican Building, a modest residential-scale structure on the U.C. Berkeley campus. Esherick was struck by the immediacy of Maybeck's working methods, and adopted a similarly spontaneous approach himself.

"He liked to draw on a chalkboard," Esherick recalls. "I'd take a drawing board over with me, paper, usually newsprint sheets, which I used to work on in those days. He didn't like that, so he asked me to get a blackboard, so I got a little blackboard at some kindergarten supply place, and he did a lot of drawings on it. Or he worked with charcoal on butcher paper, or I'd find him sketching right on the sub-floor (of a house in progress)."

Esherick's own process is similarly immediate. His initial design ideas for houses evolve directly through his interaction with clients. At each meeting, Esherick listens attentively, makes suggestions, and begins sketching as the conversation continues. Only after several sketch-and-talk sessions does he return to his office to generate polished architectural drawings.

Wurster liked to build houses from standard parts, such as inexpensive, mass-produced windows and doors. So does Esherick. He sees his biggest challenges as sculpting interior spaces and manipulating light, and is not overly concerned with what his buildings look like. The exteriors, he believes, take care of themselves if there is interior logic.

Although Esherick seems to have inherited some distinctly Maybeckian qualities—a love of materials and a disdain for publicity being two obvious ones—he stops short of crediting Maybeck as his mentor.

"In those days, we didn't know about mentors and role models," Esherick says. "I don't think the notion of a role model had been invented. We just thought he was a nice man, and as far as I was concerned, he was working with the same kinds of problems I was working on. The difference was that he had worked on them for a much longer time, and I thought his insights were important."

Esherick designed his first house in 1939 and is still designing houses at Esherick, Homsey, Dodge & Davis, the firm he founded in 1946. His houses are inconspicuous, even plain-looking, and he likes them that way. He prefers simple, rectilinear forms. His houses look boxy, but they are not simple boxes. There are always subtleties: bay windows and decks that pop out to capture views, eyebrow trellises to provide shading over windows. Windows are among his most important tools: broad windows to capture light and views for central living spaces, tall, narrow ones to admit light while maintaining privacy in bedrooms. He also likes slotlike vertical spaces that pierce through interiors, bouncing natural light down to lower floors.

Two of Esherick's favorites among the dozens of houses he's designed are the Metcalf residence at Lake Tahoe (1948) and the Cary residence in Mill Valley (1960). The former is an example of Esherick's early approach of ingeniously fitting various spaces like puzzle pieces into a straightforward shell. The Metcalf mountain house incorporates fitting materials, such as tree trunks—bark intact—used as columns. Esherick still admires the subtle play of light inside the Cary house, which came at a time when he was moving away from simpler, boxier exteriors into which he would fit various rooms to a process of design by which he allowed the layout of interior spaces to dictate exterior forms, even if they became more complex.

The McLeod house (1961) is an unpretentious shingled structure, barely visible from the street, that uses big panes of glass to make a connection to the landscape, to import daylight, and to frame panoramic views. Inside, volumes change dramatically in a carefully orchestrated sequence of interior spaces. The Bermak house (1962) has marvelously asymmetrical elevations that result from interior organization and placement of windows and shading trellises.

Despite common threads that run through generations of Bay architects, many have questioned the existence of a Bay Area Tradition. Moore, who chaired the architecture department at U.C. Berkeley from 1961 to 1965, proclaimed the death of the Bay Tradition in a chapter he contributed to Woodbridge's *Bay Area Houses*. He also questioned whether or not such a Tradition had really ever existed. Yet Moore's own work carried on some of its basic tenets, while it was also risky enough to free future generations to experiment with their own variations on local heritage. Moore developed his own poetic, eclectic style, but freely credited Bay Area architects, including Esherick and George Homsey, his fellow faculty members at Berkeley, as inspirations.

The Cary house (1960) in Mill Valley is one of Esherick's personal favorites, with interior daylighting and spatial concerns dictating exterior forms and window placement. *Bancroft Library*

Large panels of glass help Esherick's McLeod residence (1961) recede into the landscape. *Roy Flamm*

Talbert house (1962) in Oakland, designed by Moore Lyndon Turnbull Whitaker, had pop-out "saddlebags" that directly reflected its interior plan. *© Morley Baer*

Trellises shade south-facing windows at Esherick's Bermak residence (1965) and provide fine detailing that softens the overall impression. *Roy Flamm*

Sliding doors opened Moore's own tiny house in Orinda (1961) to the surrounding natural landscape. *© Morley Baer*

Moore frankly acknowledged that the idea behind his 1980 Licht house near Mill Valley was to combine Maybeck and Wurster's ideas with his own. The 1961 house Moore designed for himself in Orinda literally blew out the doors in an extreme response to its setting. Sizable corner glass barn doors slid wide open on hot days, so that indoor and outdoor spaces merged. Moore's 1962 Talbert house (a casualty of the 1991 fire) features Maybeckian vertical spaces, and Moore took Esherick's idea that interiors should define exteriors a step further, with pop-out bays and decks arranged in an assymmetrical pattern.

Architects abhor the idea of styles, of common characteristics that show up in a generation of architects as recognizable trends. In retrospect, though, it's clear that the Bay Area's top residential designers of the 1930s through 1960s were predominantly believers in Modern ideas. Through their extensive involvement with teaching architecture, Wurster and Esherick became engrossed in the clean-lined, straightforward Modern aesthetic. The influence showed up in their designs.

By the 1970s, though, younger architects were bored with the state of architecture. They found some of the buildings by their Modern-oriented elders to be cold and inhuman, and began to look for ways of injecting new life, humanity, even humor into architecture.

Moore foreshadowed the move toward a richer, more sensuous architecture with some of his 1960s Bay Area houses. By the late seventies and early eighties, architects such as Solomon were freely borrowing forms from the past, while others, including Kotas, pasted wild doodads on their buildings—to heck with pure functionalism, what about fun?

Nationally, the colorful, neoclassical, sometimes kitschy architecture that emerged during the 1980s, promoted by star architects such as Robert Venturi and Michael Graves, was labeled Postmodern. By the end of the decade, the most blatant Postmodernists, including Graves, were viewed by many architects and critics as trendmeisters whose time had come and gone. Yet the essence of what they accomplished remained. They made it okay again to design buildings that were more than boxes, to incorporate historical elements, to use color and decoration.

The nineties are under way with subtle variations on these themes. Some of the most interesting new architecture in the Bay Area and outside falls somewhere between vintage Modernism and Postmodernism. "Romantic Modernism" seems to sum up what many of these young architects are about.

Most of the new Bay Area houses included in this book emphasize the clean lines and concise spatial planning of Modernism, but add romance with color, curves, colliding volumes, and occasional decoration.

So things have come full circle. Maybeck is a desirable role model for some among the new generation, since he combined an early modern sense of space, efficiency, and experimentation with a fascination for borrowing forms from many generations of earlier buildings. Fernau and Hartman, for example, deeply admire the work of Maybeck and Esherick.

"Esherick says some interesting things," Hartman says. "He sees the Bay Tradition as a construct, more of an idea of a tradition than a formal tradition. I think it's as much a sensibility and attitude toward sites or materials as a formal, visually perceivable tradition. It's an attitude toward the land, how things are made, an awareness and sensitivity toward materials."

Others among the current crew of Bay Area architects reject the past.

"None of the Bay architects have influenced me very much," claims Saitowitz, who moved to the Bay Area from South Africa during the 1970s to attend graduate school in architecture at U.C. Berkeley. "I've never really paid much attention to their work. I'm looking at Maybeck now for the first time. My traditions are more European and Wrightean than Bay region. I would say that what one can see in Maybeck, Wright accomplished tenfold."

Saitowitz points to international architects and Los Angelenos such as Neutra, Schindler, and the brothers Eames, as some of his favorite Modern architects. Yet, of all the places he could practice, Saitowitz chooses the Bay Area.

"I think it's a nice environment to build in," he says. "I like the more experientially, rather than commercially, driven culture of northern California. There are other traditions here, in politics, in art, in theater, that are not market driven. I would say that most of what happens in Los Angeles is more commerce oriented. That tradition that led to the Beat poets and the political movements of the sixties is still powerful in northern California."

Powerful enough to make architects comfortable exploring personal and wildly diverse personal responses to the region, and to generate clients who want to experience their buildings. As Berkeley architect David Baker sees it, there is no Bay Area Tradition in the rustic sense as described by Lewis Mumford. Baker and some of his peers respect the achievements of Maybeck or Wurster or Esherick. They may borrow a form or an idea from the past masters, but they don't feel tied to some Bay Area Tradition stylistic agenda. Instead, whatever tradition there is has to do with an adventurous spirit that dates back to Gold Rush times. For whatever reason, Bay Area architects don't feel the need to band together in dogmatic theoretical groups for security, as do some of their East Coast peers.

"I think we both got interested in theoretical text, then realized there are buildings too," says Berkeley architect David Baker, whose wife, Nancy Whitcombe, is also an architect. "At some point, we just really relaxed about the whole thing. I think that's what happens to you in California, you get less pure. I think the Bay Area has been a real fertile nurturing place. You add water and things grow. A lot of things start here, and maybe they don't always reach full fruition, but it's a very good incubator."

R ustic houses designed by Bernard Maybeck and his imitators early this century established a tradition still strongly associated with the Berkeley hills. Mindful of Maybeck but also driven by wild ideas of their own, Berkeley architects David Baker and Nancy Whitcombe designed this place they call "Revenge of the Stuccoids."

It's a witty collision of old and new: an animated collection of flat-roofed stucco blocks seems to gobble the Maybeckian half of the house.

Diagonal expansion joints energize the stucco volumes. The house steps up a steep site, creating rooftop terraces that

Jutting spars of Douglas fir trellis are echoed by spiky agaves and yuccas in a terraced front garden. Alan Weintraub

Odd-shaped stucco volumes gobble the Maybeck-like portion of the house, causing Baker and Whitcombe to name their place "Revenge of the Stuccoids." Alan Weintraub

A sandstone-covered deck off the children's room offers a closer look at the Maybeck/new modern collision. Cedar board-and-batten stained mossy green recalls redwood used by Maybeck. Alan Weintraub

Baker fashioned the maple and walnut cutting board. Cooktop can be adjusted for short or tall chefs. Hearth is covered with concrete tile made by San Francisco artist Buddy Rhodes, assembled into a mosaic by artist Twyla Arthur, Whitcombe, and Baker's daughter. Alan Weintraub

Whitcombe and Baker picked up their vintage 1948 sink from a salvage yard and had the legs rechromed. Artist Twyla Arthur did the mirror and tub surrounds of Buddy Rhodes's concrete tile. The floor and walls are covered with tiny hexagonal tiles. Alan Weintraub

Whitcombe and Arthur's sandy stucco "beach wall" in the back stairwell is a sentimental piece that includes cotter pins, polishing stones, and old typesetting lead collected by Arthur's late father, along with Whitcombe's shells. Frames around slot windows are dusted with bronze powder. Alan Weintraub

become outdoor extensions of rooms. Living areas for Baker, Whitcombe, and two children flow casually together, with the kitchen, dining, and living rooms in the open core and a home studio off the living room. Several rooms have views across the Bay to San Francisco and the Golden Gate.

The plan is a merger of traditional Maybeckian rectangular shapes and skittering, off-kilter squares of the stuccoids. Out of this teetering plan grew two fallaway walls, one on the front of the kitchen, the other at the back of the main stairwell.

Baker was a carpenter before he became an architect, and he designed the aluminum benches that wrap the entry porch, built the wood cutting board and cabinets in the kitchen, and handled numerous other finish details. Baker's daughter, Whitcombe, and Bay Area artist Twyla Arthur laid mosaics of fractured tile on the kitchen counter and hearth and in the master bath, and Arthur added multihued tile borders around bathroom mirrors.

Baker and Whitcombe both earned master's degrees from U.C. Berkeley, and their architecture has grown progressively looser as they become more confident. Their designs are definitely experimental, pushing toward fresh responses to Bay Area conditions, but don't expect houses like this one to lead to a singular manifesto.

"The important thing about rules is, break them!" Baker says.

San Francisco's steep, narrow lots bring out the worst in some architects. The city's hills are overrun with legions of banal, boxy row houses.

These same lots are San Francisco architect Jeremy Kotas's creative playground. Since the late 1970s, Kotas, an alumni of progressive architect Frank Gehry, of the Los Angeles office, has been on a romp, reinventing the row house again and again.

"There are purists, whether antiquarians or Modernists, who like their row houses lined up like little soldiers," says Kotas, a former city planner in San Francisco. "I think the military metaphor is a terrible one for a city."

Kotas steps out of formation with vivid colors, inspired uses of common materials, and kinetic forms, yet he keeps basic row house rules in mind.

In the past, his designs challenged the traditional sensibilities of some neighbors and city planners. But this house, which marks a new, more restrained phase in Kotas's work, sailed smoothly to completion.

The architects dubbed it the "House of Faith," in honor of its owner, a schoolteacher named Faith. Kotas and his partner, Anthony Pantaleoni, and staff architect Joanne Koch, responded to their client's request for a Modern house that would be

The front bay, covered with bent plywood, cranes for a better look at the downtown skyline. The house is Kotas's update of classic San Francisco row houses. Richard Barnes

A blank side wall preserves privacy, but a notch admits extra daylight. A yellow entry bay and Plexiglas awning are visible to left. Richard Barnes

Kotas manipulated angles and forms to make the compact living room at the front of the house seem larger. Deep recesses help dignify economical aluminum windows. Richard Barnes

A central skylit spine runs through the house from front to back on the main level, sweeping from the living room past the red entry door to the kitchen and dining spaces. Richard Barnes

A fabric screen adds privacy to a small rear deck, braced by five diagonal redwood struts. Richard Barnes

"out of the ordinary, but not too weird," and a homey place for her grown sons to spend some weekends.

The 25-foot-wide lot came from Faith's elderly mother, who lives next door. To preserve privacy for both Faith and her mom, the uphill wall facing mom's place is gray and blank, save for a small triangular window that admits natural light. Popping out from the stucco, the plywood ends of the house, stained bright yellow, crane to capture views of the downtown

skyline and Mt. Diablo, with a sweep reminiscent of an Aalto chair.

Inside, a simple but subtle open plan encourages easy movement between rooms and makes this 1800-square-foot house seem bigger. Three 4-foot-square skylights disperse daylight down a main entry hall that connects second-floor kitchen, living, and dining rooms. A garage, guest room, bathroom, and garden-facing workroom occupy the ground floor.

Among its conventional row-house neighbors, the house seems like an anomaly, yet it shares many of their principles.

Typical San Francisco row houses, Kotas notes, consist of bases that marry the buildings to their steep, uneven sites; long, narrow living spaces above; and "attachments" including bay windows, various roof forms, and assorted decorations.

The House of Faith has a base and exterior walls of gray cement plaster, with red stones embedded in the plaster that will gradually be exposed as the house weathers. Yellow projections front and back denote the ends of the narrow living envelope. A Plexiglas awning over

the entry and a saillike fabric screen that shelters the rear deck are "attachments" that animate the exterior, along with a roof that kicks up like an airplane wing on takeoff.

One of Kotas's heroes is turn-of-the-century San Francisco architect Ernest Coxhead. Many San Francisco row houses designed by Coxhead still stand and are characterized by witty illusions of scale and surprising combinations of forms.

Kotas's affection for Coxhead-like illusions can be seen in the House of Faith's living room, a compact space made to seem larger and extra cozy by its high ceiling and oversized fireplace. Another ingenious bit of deception is the way economical aluminum front windows gain depth and weight from the shadows of their deep-set openings.

There is a word Kotas uses to describe his creations: syncretic.

"That's when you take two or more things of incompatible nature and fuse them together at white hot heat," he explains, "so they become something else and rise above what they were."

Mediterranean culture, from architecture to vineyards, has been imported to California for many generations. Architects Steven and Cathi House have traveled extensively throughout the Mediterranean, documenting buildings and details in their search for inspiration. This major remodel for a physician, his design-conscious wife, and four young children is House + House's fresh take on Mediterrean courtyard dwellings.

Largely invisible from the street, where the home's original Tudor facade blends with the traditional suburban neighborhood, the pastel-hued addition behind provides a dynamic contrast. The new wing was added to the original U-shaped structure to enclose a central courtyard lined with pinkish Cantera stone, with a fountain visible from the new entrance. The addition includes expansive new living and dining rooms and an island kitchen open to a family room. These first-floor rooms flow easily from one to another, without conventional hallways.

A new, secluded second-level master bedroom suite has a glass block wall that admits light and greenish plant impressions from the garden, and a master bath with a purple neon-ringed walk-in shower. Children's bedrooms occupy the original wing.

A new entry unites the new portion of the house at left with the original structure to the right. Vertical slit windows admit natural light to the living/dining space inside. Alan Weintraub

A vaulted circulation element enters on a diagonal from the back. A second-level glass block wall floods the master bedroom with light. Doors off the kitchen open to a back terrace. Alan Weintraub

The courtyard scheme was inspired by House + House's travels through several Mediterranean countries. Pavers are pinkish Cantera stone. Alan Weintraub

The copper-and-concrete fireplace designed by House + House jolts the living-dining space with kinetic angles and curves. Alan Weintraub

Bold elements serve as focal points in the design. A cylindrical tower contains the first-floor dining nook and master shower. A two-story skylit corridor slices into a corner of the house on a diagonal, and a stucco wall arcs across one end of the courtyard, tying together the old and new wings.

The architects designed furnishings to suit the angular, dynamic architecture, including a boldly sculpted copper-and-concrete fireplace, Douglas fir kitchen cabinets stained trans-parent green, black granite countertops, and several pieces of furniture. They also helped the owners select contemporary furnishings to go with existing pieces by designers such as Le Corbusier and Charles Rennie Mackintosh.

Spacious and dramatic, the home is also casual and inti-mate. The courtyard is the social hub, a place where the children dance to rap music piped in from a sophisticated sound system, also a place where their parents host large parties. The kitchen/family complex is the family hub, where listening to music, read-ing, or watching television are options while waiting for infor-mal meals, while the master suite offers a private, luxurious escape hatch.

Although the house is color-ful and kinetic, its varied ele-ments are bound together by rigorous geometric logic. This underlying order seamlessly unites the past with the present.

A curved wall runs along the edge of the courtyard, defining a hall that connects dining and family rooms. Alan Weintraub

The kitchen has cabinets of green-stained Douglas fir and counters covered with black granite. The dining room at the far end occupies the base of a cylindrical tower at the back corner of the house. Alan Weintraub

A split-level stair leads up from the kitchen to a vaulted second-level circulation spine. Alan Weintraub

A walk-in master shower is ringed by a halo of recessed neon.
Alan Weintraub

TANNER LEDDY MAYTUM STACY
RICHARD STACY

Cool, efficient, and metallic, this three-level live/work loft sheds new light on that old cliché, "living machine." Meticulously designed by San Francisco architect Richard Stacy, the building is both home and office to fashion photographer Thomas Heinser and his wife, graphic designer Madeline Corson.

Design-conscious by training, the couple was immediately enthusiastic when Stacy, a partner at Tanner Leddy Maytum Stacy, proposed this spare, industrial-strength building for a 20-by-75-foot lot in San Francisco's south-of-Market Street warehouse district. A dedicated Modernist, Stacy believes his buildings can address the special qualities of the Bay region without drawing literally on earlier precedents.

In keeping with Stacy's philosophy, the Heinser/Corson loft doesn't look like a classic Bay building, yet it extends Bay traditions of simple materials used honestly and daylight carefully manipulated.

The exterior is a straightforward expression of what's inside. Stacy grouped all service features—stairs, bathrooms, and a dumbwaiter—on the south, leaving the north side free for uncluttered living and working spaces. Galvanized sheet metal panels define the utilitarian service side, while broad banks of aluminum windows identify living and working spaces. On the front facade, a narrow vertical strip of stained marine plywood marks the line between the two.

Plywood sheer walls on the ends of the building would not have allowed sufficient window area, so Stacy used steel frames, which enhance earthquake safety. Instead of hiding the steel under another finish material, as is common, he exposed it to define the exterior. Other durable, affordable exterior materials include steel mesh panels and quarter-inch-thick cement boards.

In laying out the interior, Heinser's need for natural light for his photography won out over the convenience of ground-floor access, so his studio went on the top floor. The couple's living loft takes up the entire second floor and a garage and Corson's studio share the first floor.

Heinser's work space is flooded with daylight that streams in through skylights, vertical and horizontal side windows, and the big bank of glass at the front of the building. Corson's studio, at the back of the building, looks out on a pocket garden through an industrial roll-up door she keeps wide open on warm days.

The couple's wide-open living space features an affordable, functional floor of particle

Stacy used a spare, machinelike aesthetic in keeping with the industrial character of the urban neighborhood. Heinser and Courson's steely new live/work loft butts up against an older building.
Thomas Heinser

board panels, and efficient ship-like galley kitchen with stainless steel counters, and a bedroom that can be closed off with sliding shoji-like panels.

Heinser finds the building a comfortable place to live and work, and a useful marketing tool in his dealing with corporate clients, who get a kick out of visiting his studio for meetings.

"They enjoy being thrown into a different world," he says.

Steel stairs rise through the core of the building, drawing daylight from adjacent living areas through Plexiglas clerestories. Thomas Heinser

Heinser and Corson's second-level living space has a long galley kitchen with stainless-steel counters. Thomas Heinser

Corson's studio at the back of the ground floor opens wide to a pocket patio. Thomas Heinser

Shoji-like sliding panels close off the bedroom from the rest of the living space. Thomas Heinser

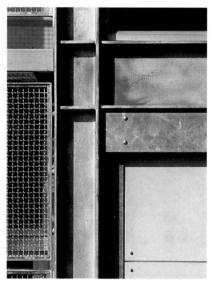

Materials aren't typical of the Bay Area, but they are put together with a degree of care that runs back through several generations of Bay Area architecture.
Thomas Heinser

San Francisco architect Mark Mack generally finds the Bay Area a conservative and confining place to work. In fact, Mack, who was born in Austria and has practiced in the Bay Area since 1978, is gradually shifting his focus to southern California, which he believes is more open to fresh ideas. In the case of this unusual and extensive remodel, though, he was captivated by a chance to reshape a vernacular relic in the Berkeley hills into a modern dwelling for a family with two young children.

The original house was built during the 1960s by Judd Boynton, a designer and builder whose mother, a dancer, owned the "Temple of the Wings," a dramatic neoclassical courtyard home designed by Bernard Maybeck in 1914. Exposed to the arts and architecture at an early age, Boynton went on to build several homes of rough-sawn wood beams and board-formed concrete in the hills behind U.C. Berkeley. This one, completed during the 1960s, was his last.

When acquired by Mack's clients, Jim and Laura Baum, Boynton's earthy enclave consisted of a cavernous main living space under a ceiling supported by gigantic wood beams, a kitchen, a bathroom shed, plus two small bedrooms with a second bath. The house also came with an incredible hilltop site

Mack used straightforward stucco and concrete in keeping with Boynton's original buildings, but added color that contrasts with the earthy landscape and energizes the new buildings. Richard Barnes

A new kitchen/dining space were of yellow wood and concrete was added to Boynton's original great room, visible at left. Richard Barnes

overlooking the university campus and San Francisco Bay.

Initially, Mack was not impressed with Boynton's efforts. The concrete work was expert, Mack says, but in other ways the buildings were loosely crafted. In time, however, Mack came to appreciate them as important links in the chain of local architectural history.

"Board-formed concrete was used by Maybeck and Julia Morgan during the twenties and thirties," he says. "To me it's a very significant element for the region, both for its innovation and its primitiveness. Judd Boynton's house captured a California spirit."

With the original great room serving as the core of his new design, Mack nearly doubled the home's living area while retaining Boynton's con-

New wings of the house enclose a grass courtyard. Richard Barnes

crete foundation and walls and hefty wood beams. Mack added some new concrete pads and board-formed concrete walls to match's Boynton's originals, but

A new kitchen flows into Boynton's great room, with its concrete floor and giant lam beams. Richard Barnes

Mack's addition is distinguished by bold new volumes wrapped in smooth, vibrantly colored stucco.

Facing the street, a new red garage/guest room wing rises above a concrete base. Out front, steps lead up from the driveway to an entry under a flying section of roof tethered by a single concrete column. For privacy's sake, this south-facing facade has only two windows,

lending a Mediterranean mystique.

Boynton's original main room remains largely as it was, situated on the west side, with its cantilevered floor jutting toward the bay beyond broad expanses of glass. These windows frame stunning views and strengthen the relationship between the interior and the surrounding natural landscape. A sizable grass courtyard and a smaller

pocket patio are integrated into the floorplan as usable outdoor "rooms." These encourage casual, easy movement between indoor and outdoor spaces, a longstanding California tradition.

Mack's simple, open plan unites old and new spaces. Boynton's original main hallway was extended to sweep through the house from the sleek new kitchen at the south to a new

Mack supervised the tinting and smooth-troweling of the salmon-colored wall in the master bedroom. Richard Barnes

studio office at the north, past three bedrooms in between. The largest of these is a master suite featuring a board-formed concrete fireplace and a reddish plaster wall at the head of the bed, smooth troweled, under Mack's watchful eye, by workers who sprinkled on water tinted with the same pigment used on the exterior.

While earlier Bay Area architects such as Maybeck pre-ferred subtle colors that harmonized with natural settings, Mack has a different philsophy, evident in the bold yellow, red, and blue he used inside and out on the Baum residence.

"A house can stand up against nature rather than be in sync with it," he says. "There is a sort of duality and tension that can be exploited. If you have a very green environment and you pick opposing colors such as red or orange, they bring out the landscape as well as the house."

The Baum residence proves that even an architect such as Mack, who has strong ideas of his own and feels hampered by local pressures toward conservative, familiar design, has a soft spot for some Bay traditions.

A tiled master bath runs along one of Boynton's original concrete walls. Richard Barnes

Boynton's original great room cantilevers boldly westward, toward a dramatic Bay Area view. Richard Barnes

Architects David Weingarten and Lucia Howard of Ace Architects in Oakland don't subscribe to the most familiar Bay Area tradition of unassuming, woodsy houses, but they *do* feel drawn to other area precedents.

This Arabian fantasy, which Weingarten and Howard have dubbed "Xanadu," harks back to the eclecticism of Bernard Maybeck and Julia Morgan, early twentieth century Bay Area architects who drew imaginatively from a variety of historical sources, and to their peers Ernest Coxhead, W.R. Yelland, and John Hudson Thomas, less well known, but equally adept at deploying historical references.

Bold, graphic, and playful, Ace's work is the antithesis of cool, minimal Modernism. Weingarten and Howard enjoy combining historical forms familiar to many people and therefore charged with romantic emotional potential. In this case, their clients, a couple with three children, hired Weingarten and Howard to redo a nondescript 1940s dwelling on a challenging hillside lot with a dramatic view across downtown Oakland and San Francisco Bay to the skyline of San Francisco.

Prompted by the couple's fascination with Arabian buildings and fables about Sinbad's adventures, the architects let their imaginations run wild to create this colorful assemblage of Islamic arches, columns, clover-like "trefoils," domes, minarets, towers, and polychromatic tile mosaics. In the process, they doubled the three-level home's living area, added two bedrooms to the existing three, and gave a friendly, open layout to the main family living space on the second floor.

A domed entry tower hails visitors like an Islamic mosque gone wild with copper columns and beams carved with dragonheads. The sheet-metal dome came from a supplier to Midwestern farmers who use the domes to cap grain silos. A recessed Moorish arch at the tower's base frames a sky-blue front door bordered by tiny gold tiles in a field of blue. It's a threshold that hints at magic and mystery within.

From each vantage point inside, architectural dramas beckon. Flooded with daylight from a circular skylight in its dome, the cylindrical entry foyer opens on the heart of the house: an expansive kitchen/dining/living room space filled with custom cabinets, chairs, and tables designed by the architects using forms that echo the architecture. Off the living room is an octagonal family room the architects call the "pleasure dome," crowned with another silo dome. French doors open to a balcony that

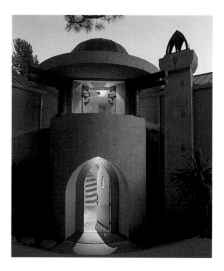

Ace's Turkish fantasy has a domed entry tower with dragonhead rafter tails and an Islamic arch. Alan Weintraub

juts off the back of this cozy room like a ship's prow straining toward the distant bay.

Along with recurring forms and consistently high-quality craftsmanship that Maybeck might admire, color is what holds this assemblage together. Weingarten and Howard credit a 1930s guide to historic revival color schemes for helping them achieve this unlikely but entirely pleasing palette of red, orange, sky blue, and cream.

The house captures some of the theatrical spirit of turn-of-the-century Berkeley, when artistic types would gather at unusual and majestic settings such as Maybeck's outdoor "Temple of the Wings" (de-

Tiny gold tiles form a cosmic spiral on the entry floor. Spiral copper columns rise through the tower. Alan Weintraub

stroyed in the 1923 fire) for afternoons of dance and pageantry.

"Family life is ritualized to some extent," Weingarten says. "This house is a theatrical setting that encourages a fresh and spontaneous way of living. It's much more fun to gather guests on pillows and divans under the 'pleasure dome' than to seat them on a couch in the 'family room.'"

The trefoil pattern on chairbacks repeats architectural forms. Alan Weintraub

Ace repeated Islamic arches on custom furniture. Alan Weintraub

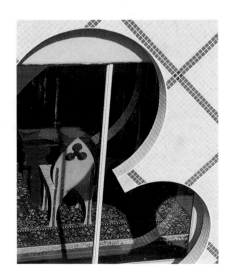

Beyond the trefoil blue-tile window scrim, the glass dining table is etched with a pattern circumscribed by an unbroken line, an Arabic symbol. Alan Weintraub

S an Francisco architect Stanley Saitowitz sees his buildings as products of nature, growing logically out of each site. He calls his architecture "geologic," and writes about "mining" the earth for materials he can use to make spaces that "extend the exuberant parts of life."

For a site on a lagoon at Stinson Beach, just up the California coast from San Francisco, Saitowitz designed a house that

Curving in from the street, a wall of cedar clapboards wraps the north side of the house, and the roof kicks up like ocean waves off Stinson Beach. Richard Barnes

Saitowitz angled the deck away from the shoreline so the primary view is down the lagoon, instead of across at other houses. Richard Barnes

The sweeping roof seems to float atop a band of glass. Richard Barnes

A horizontal strip window in the street-facing kitchen admits extra daylight while maintaining privacy. The front door is behind the kitchen. Richard Barnes

expresses his organic philosophy. Sheathed in wood that will weather with the elements, crafted into wavelike curves, it is the perfect place to contemplate the vast, ever-changing coastal landscape.   In autumn, for instance, mist shrouds low lion's fur mountains in the distance, gray clouds scud across the sky, and wind off the ocean bends tawny grass and ripples the lagoon.

Saitowitz describes the house as if he were a naturalist leading a beach walk:

"The roof—a wave—reflects the nearby but absent ocean. The space—a cave—is carved out by water. Shell-like, the outside is a driftwood crust, protecting an iridescent interior charged with sunlight."

Saitowitz's plan relates to both natural and man-made geometries. The central circula-

tion spine aligns with the parallel road and lagoon, but front and back walls cut across on a diagonal. The house is open to the southwest, with most of its glass and a wide rear deck facing the lagoon.

Privacy is provided by a front wall of cedar clapboards that curves in from the street to the lagoon, wrapping the north side of the house, with horizontal strip windows and a larger tri-

*Glass between walls and roof is butted
pane to pane, held in place by simple
wood stops. Richard Barnes*

angular window providing daylight.

Construction cost was kept
below $100,000 because the
owner, a contractor, handled
much of the work. Saitowitz
selected simple, economical
materials and found provocative
ways to put them together.
Glass panels are inserted
between the roof and walls without conventional frames, held
in place by simple wood stops.
Economical round steel col-

umns at the edge of the kitchen
eliminate the need for a load-
bearing wall, opening up the
interior. Bowed, laminated
wood beams support the flying
roof. Panels of Medite, a type of
particle board, are used as flooring, coated with polyurethane
and screwed to joists, the screws
left exposed.

Intimately related to nature,
the house recalls the earthiness
of wood houses by earlier Bay
Area architects.

"Living in a particular
region, there's a palette of materials and technologies that are
available," Saitowitz says. "If you
live in Boston, you build out of
brick. Using wood is a practical
way to build in northern California, but that doesn't make this
Bay Regionalist architecture.
I'm not interested in styles. 'Bay
Region' is a style. I'm more
interested in the particular character of sites."

Dark and cool-looking, this house designed by San Francisco architect Daniel Solomon makes a Darth Vadar-like initial impression. But while its black asphalt shingle exterior seems chiseled from a block of solid obsidian, the interior is open and inviting and changes moods with the weather and time of day.

Solomon's clients were partners in the design process. Joan Jeanrenaud is a member of the Kronos String Quartet. Her husband, Patrick Gleeson, composes music for movies and television on elaborate electronic equipment.

"We worked with Dan like a bunch of jazz musicians," says Gleeson, describing design meetings as loose, spontaneous jam sessions that yielded maximum creativity.

"The house shines with Pat's personality and tastes," Solomon says. "He came to me with a little drawing and said, 'You may not want to work on this house, because it's all designed.' Well, most everything that was in his sketch is in the house. I very much enjoy working with strong, creative

Solomon is not above playful allusions to the past, such as minimalist flattened bay windows that draw on a long San Francisco tradition of view- and light-catching bays. Dominic Vorillon

Stairs spiral up from first-floor garage through the core of the house around a post topped with a '56 Chevy headlamp. Natural light spills down from a round Plexiglas skylight. Dominic Vorillon

Perforated steel panels cover living room walls. Interior furnishings strike a balance between cool grays and warmer brown tones.
Dominic Vorillon

Kitchen cabinets and counters are covered with zinc, a second-level hallway in the split-level central space leads to the master bath. Dominic Vorillon

people who have an informed sense of what they want to do."

The house is on a steep street that climbs San Francisco's Potrero Hill.

"Potrero Hill has its own character in the city," Solomon says. "It's less consistent, less prim and polite, more accommodating of mischief, funkiness, artiness, idiosyncracy than other parts of the city. People like Pat and Joan are drawn to it because it is a slightly rough,

partly industrial, partly residential city edge."

Solomon designed a house that strikes a balance between cool precision and warmth. In the simplest of terms, the house is a cube pierced by a cylindrical light and circulation well, set atop a base of exposed concrete block. Gleeson and Jeanrenaud's music dictated the interior layout.

"The plan comes out of the acoustic form of the two stu-

dios," Solomon says. Gleeson's friend, John Storyk, an expert music studio designer, conceived the two rooms with high ceilings and nonparallel walls. "We had two odd-shaped things that are the same size, and the rest of the plan flows from that," Solomon explains.

Solomon tucked the studios at the back of the house, flanking the entry. To get to the "front" door, you climb steps up one side of the house and cross a spare back landscape of crushed granite and concrete stepping stones. Studios look out on this landscape through sliding doors.

Gleeson and Jeanrenaud had strong feelings about the forms the interior should take. They are most comfortable in wide-open living spaces.

"We lived in warehouses for so many years, and it made me dislike the scale of most residential structures," Gleeson says. "They're too tight."

The kitchen and living room are combined into one large space at the heart of the house, with a fireplace set into the tall front window wall of glass, flanked by Solomon's variation on San Francisco bay windows. The bays rise up the full height of the front wall, supplying natural light for both the living room and the upper-level master bedroom and bath, loft-like spaces open to the living room and connected by a bridgelike hallway.

After living in the Bay Area for several years, Gleeson says he is "real sick of redwood. Dan and I share an interest in despised materials." Gleeson

Truss joists supporting the ceiling were ordered from an industrial parts catalog. The loftlike master bedroom looks down on the living room. *Dominic Vorillon*

Jeanrenaud's acoustical sound studio has spiral stairs that lead to her office loft. *Dominic Vorillon*

originally wanted to cover interior walls with ripply white plastic used on greenhouses, but gave up that idea when he found out the material is highly flammable. Instead, walls are covered with perforated steel panels or smooth-troweled stucco, the ceiling above the double-height central living space is supported by wood-and-steel truss joists ordered from an industrial building parts catalog, and zinc lines counters, cabinets, and interior doors.

Oak floors and wood furniture lend a soft, natural touch.

Interior designer Terry Hunziker added furnishings and fabrics in gray, charcoal, and warmer brown tones.

Solomon's home for Gleeson and Jeanrenaud is like nothing the San Francisco hills have seen, but Solomon conceived it as an abstraction of familiar local elements, and as a house tailored to a specific site and specific clients.

"It doesn't have bay windows that are like other people's bay windows, but it has them," he says of his flattened bays. "It doesn't have redwood or cedar

shingles, but it has shingles. So it is a sort of set of inverted references to what's around it. My view of doing what's appropriate to a place does not include replicating other buildings. Pat and Joan's house is different from what's around it, but I couldn't imagine building the same house anywhere else."

Fog drifts eerily through tall oak trees surrounding the Napa Valley home Helen Berggruen shares with another artist. On a chilly December morning, there's not a trace of wind, but yellow and orange leaves drift down anyway with a steady rainlike pitter-patter.

Farther from the house are acres of vineyards. This is classic northern California wine country, a rural setting that inspired Berkeley architects Richard Fernau and Laura Hartman to design this string of shedlike buildings between two creekbeds.

Fernau and Hartman often draw on vernacular architecture surrounding a site, and their houses can seem hauntingly familiar. But each house is also a fresh expression of what the architects learn about individual clients and sites. Materials may be common but they are used in uncommon ways. The architects are committed to designing buildings that are rich and not easily summarized.

Berggruen is an artist whose oil paintings fill her compact studio atop the tower. Her most recent pictures depict rooms that look out on landscapes alive with color and undulating motion, capturing some of the raw power of her wine country milieu. The house suits Berggruen's basic day-to-day existence: painting, writing, reading, fixing

meals, and it's also a great place for entertaining.

The architects drew initial inspiration from old wood-and-tin cabins that previously occupied the site. The new tower and living areas are configured in an *L* around a gravel court, with an opening in the tower's base that allows pickup trucks to deliver firewood or haul off yard debris. A detached secondary studio at the front of the site and an outdoor fireplace pavilion at the back serve as bookends for the main buildings.

Berggruen's studio in the top of the tower has views of surrounding vineyards and distant rolling hills. Her second-level tower bedroom consists mainly of a compact bed wedged within three walls, with a view of vineyards to the south.

A section of green metal roof slants above a staircase connecting the tower to Berggruen's office, which shares the main building with the living room and kitchen. These rooms are separately defined, but connected by large openings.

A vine-covered pergola joins the kitchen to a detached guest bedroom.

Exterior materials are concrete block, galvanized iron, and wood painted green, red, and yellow, with different combinations defining the parts of the house. Roof forms help delineate these parts: an invert-

The friendly jumble of forms was inspired by the original wood-and-tin shacks on site. Christopher Irion

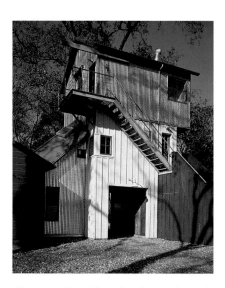

Berggruen's studio takes the top floor of the entry tower. Christopher Irion

ed shed roof above the living room, dormers over the kitchen, and a hipped roof atop the detached bedroom.

Interiors were scaled for the women who live and work in the house. Stairs and some doorways are narrower than normal and rooms are relatively small, lending a sense of enclosure

A pocket reading room beyond off Berggruen's office is one of a few cozy bonus spaces. Each room is identified by different roof forms. Artists Mandy Wallace and Maria McVarish painted patterned wainscotings on walls. Christopher Irion

Living in the house has inspired some of Berggruen's paintings, such as this view of her pergola and guest bunkhouse. Sutro

The compact kitchen catches a glimpse of the courtyard. Fernau and Hartman use windows with restraint and place them carefully to frame views. Christopher Irion

Forms are fresh, colors are lively, but with its modest, varied profile, the house recedes into its grove of old oak trees. Christopher Irion

that seems especially comforting during winter months, when a woodburning stove in the living room is the primary heat source. Fernau and Hartman favor selective use of windows to frame specific views, rather than uninterrupted expanses of glass. Since the house is only one room deep, each room gets natural light from several directions.

Berggruen is not given to hyperbole, but she comes alive when talking about her house.

"Every time you look out a window, something is framed in a way that is very exciting or pleasing," she says. "The coziness is very nice, but you also have the sense, in a relatively small space, of openness, because the open plan lets rooms borrow space from each other."

Regionalism, for Fernau and Hartman, is about responding to circumstances, not perpetuating a style, although some of their houses have similarities such as dynamic collaging of

forms and materials and selective use of intense color to define and energize individual volumes.

"The Berggruen house is tied to the specific situation, in the sense that it couldn't be anywhere else, responding to the climate, the topography, the views, the client," Hartman says. "Earlier Bay Area buildings were also very site-specific, and we feel connected to the past, but it's more a linkage of attitude than any sort of direct reference."

LOS ANGELES

RETROSPECTIVE

LA

Schindler's 1922 Hollywood house marks the passage of each day with movement of light and shadow. Dominic Vorillon

A daylong pilgrimage past shrines of Modern residential architecture in Los Angeles takes you to houses by the brothers Greene, Richard Neutra, the Wrights, John Lautner, Ray and Charles Eames, and other twentieth-century innovators. But it is the place that R. M. Schindler built for himself on Kings Road in Hollywood in 1922 that resonates through your memory as you head home, tired and overwhelmed.

With his modest composition in concrete, glass, and redwood, Schindler made a leap in perceiving southern California's special qualities and addressing them in architecture. He was enough ahead of his time that the house was not appreciated by historians, architects, and design editors until several years later. Quietly innovative, the building has an enduring grace and raw power. Many of the city's young architects today find inspiration in Schindler's work, especially this building.

On weekends, Greene and Greene's Gamble house (1908) in Pasadena and Frank Lloyd Wright's Hollyhock house (1917 to 1920) in Hollywood are full of tourists, cameras draped around their necks as they ooh and ah at rich detailing. But the Schindler house is packed with architecture students, sketching Schindler's plan, running their hands over the concrete, standing in the middle of each of the four studios to marvel at the play of natural light from several directions.

The Schindler house, open to the public, is creaky now. The roof leaks, even after an expensive replacement, steps to second-level sleeping porches wobble, and sections of concrete are cracking. Still, the house stands as a testament to Schindler's experimental nature and his determination to design a more purely California house, one that would respond to the light, the weather, the open lay of the then undeveloped land, using materials available on the West Coast.

With advice from San Diego architect Irving Gill, who was on site during construction, Schindler had concrete panels poured flat on the ground and tilted into place as walls, with vertical strips of glass in between to let in daylight. The plan grew out of Schindler's openness to alternative lifestyles, an attitude that was progressive for his time but has become essential today, with changing social structures and fracturing families. Schindler's house has four studios for four

Sliding panels open the interior of Schindler's home wide to the court, while tilt-up concrete walls gave privacy from the street. Julius Shulman

Clerestories, vertical slit windows, banks of windows provide natural light from several directions. Each room has a fireplace. Julius Shulman

artists—Schindler, his wife, Pauline, and another couple, the Chases—with a central communal kitchen and courtyard gardens shared by each L-shaped pair of studios.

Spatially, the Schindler house was innovative for California, although Wright had employed open plans and carefully orchestrated progressions of interior volumes for several years. If you have only seen Schindler's house in wide-angle photos in books, you will be surprised by how small it looks in person. But the scale is deceptive. The eaves are low, the wide door openings to the courtyards barely six feet tall. Step inside, however, and space explodes. Ceilings pop up to eight and one half feet above clerestories, rooms seem larger than they are because of the way space extends outside, and the open plan makes an inviting, casual impression.

Space would be nothing without light, and the Schindler house tracks the course of a California day like a finely tuned three-dimensional sundial. In the morning, golden light slants in through narrow strip windows to cast glowing bars across concrete floors covered with simple seisel mats. By noon, the sun is higher and hotter and its light filters in through clerestories to stripe the floor and simple wood furniture designed by Schindler. Indirect daylight streams in through glazed corners that help make the rectangular studios feel light and open.

Despite his endless advocacy of cross ventilation, Schindler failed to provide any on Kings Road. He later retrofitted operable clerestories; these have been returned to original form, and in mid-summer the house can be stifling, without a trace of breeze.

Stay until evening and you'll see the house at its finest, when it is most like the Yosemite campground that provided a portion of Schindler's inspiration (he learned the drama of fireplaces from Wright, his mentor), with protective walls at your back and open views of nature in front of you. Some nights, visitors light fires in any of seven fireplaces inside and out and shadows bounce off the concrete walls to signal the end of another day. You can imagine Schindler climbing up the narrow steps to one of the sleeping porches to dream dreams of further adventures in concrete.

Schindler's houses, like Frank Lloyd Wright's 1920s concrete block houses, and the later Case Study Houses, were attempts to come to terms with the city's complex personality, to find architectural expression uniquely suited to the southern California region.

The notion of regional architecture presses different buttons in different people. Some young architects in Los Angeles in the 1990s—"young" meaning in their thirties or forties—view regionalism as a valid concept. To them, southern California has individual characteristics such as climate and certain types of terrain that produce unique buildings. Some of these architects admire Schindler, or Ain, or Gill, or others who came before them, for their sensitivity to L.A.'s idiosyncracies. But there are other architects who feel that the idea of regionalism is too narrow, that in Los Angeles, architecture has long been as national and international in its sources as it is regional.

"What's regional anyway?" muses L.A. architect Eric Owen Moss. "Is it California? Lots of people look on L.A. as the center of discussion of architectural ideas. Other people want to compare Los Angeles with Europe, or Italy versus Austria, or Milano versus Napoli, or my block versus your block.

"What Schindler was doing certainly has antecedents in other places, from Chicago to Japan. If he was regionalist in some ways, he was also international, part of a general movement. It isn't necessarily one or the other. If you're interested in the (regionalist) question beyond a cartoon level, I think a lot of the work now done in the world is inevitably the consequence of the association of people from place to place. Japanese come to America, Americans go to Europe, Europeans to Japan. I think Schindler was part of that relatively early."

The challenge of designing a house for any of Los Angeles's distinct locations, from the flat Venice beachfront to the low ocean-view hills of Santa Monica Canyon to the Hollywood Hills and the hills overlooking Silverlake, in a city also defined by the predominance of the auto, the miracle of imported water, and complex cultural and artistic forces, has perplexed many a gifted architect.

Since the Greenes designed their first California bungalows in Pasadena around the turn of the century, Los Angeles has been a laboratory for experimental architecture by Gill, Lautner, the Wrights, Neutra, Gregory Ain, Harwell Hamilton Harris, Raphael Soriano, Craig Ellwood, the Case Study architects, Ray Kappe, Frank Gehry, and many others.

The pace has quickened since Gehry's radical remodel of his own Santa Monica home in 1978, with a subsequent generation of architects—the primary subjects of this book—coming up behind him. Instead of looking to an ideology, such as Modernism, or searching for a purely regional architecture tailored to southern California's climate, light, and available materials, Gehry, who has acknowledged that art is an important inspiration, made it acceptable to approach architecture as sculpture that could function both as dwelling and art object.

He found his own ways to relate houses to their neighborhoods, as with his 1983 Norton beach house, with its lifeguard towerlike office overlooking the Venice boardwalk, and he elevated industrial materials such as corrugated metal, wire-reinforced glass, and chain-link fencing to the status of residential construction. Critics of Gehry and a few other younger L.A. architects charge that they have sacrificed sensitivity to sites and surrounding terrain, and often forsaken integral connections between indoor and outdoor space, in order to make strong graphic statements with their buildings.

That's not the case with Melinda Gray, who designed a Santa Monica Canyon house included in this book. She worked for Eric Moss and inherited some of his wild, experimental nature. She is obsessed with intricate, controlled geometric plans and well-proportioned exteriors, but she also makes intelligent use of carefully placed courtyards, gardens, balconies, and other outdoor spaces that serve as visual and circulation extensions of interiors.

Frank Israel, whose Goldberg-Bean residence is pictured in this book, has developed a formally aggressive, colorful approach to design, but he also integrates houses with their sites and landscaping. Israel's houses are obviously influenced by Schindler in their intimate in/out connections, multidirectional daylighting, and expressed structural systems, but Israel is more dedicated to craftsmanship than Schindler.

Julie Eizenberg and Hank Koning's own Santa Monica house, included here, has a sliding window-wall that opens the main living space to the garden, beyond a vine-covered trellis, a sequence of spaces that speaks of many earlier California houses. But the plan of their house is also drawn from vernacular houses they've seen in Virginia and in their native Australia. Josh Schweitzer admits his devotion to Schindler, but the trapezoidal window openings and intense colors he employed at his Joshua Tree house show the liberating influence of Gehry. Jay Vanos, who works for Moss and designs houses on his own, shares some of Moss's fascination with complex, energetic forms. Vanos' own house, snuggled into the lushness of Topanga Canyon, combines dynamic sculptural forms with inventive use of materials that suit the textures and colors of the site.

W hether or not you buy into the idea of regionalism in California's Modern architecture, it is possible to trace some common threads back from today through earlier decades, to the work of the Greene brothers, Henry Mather, and Charles Sumner. While the Greenes' houses seem too rustic to be considered Modern in a stylistic sense, the brothers shared a few basic Arts and Crafts ideals with Gill and Schindler, true Moderns who distanced themselves eventually from the Craftsman style.

Dedicated to architecture as a force for healthier living, an idea that was promoted in England by the Arts and Crafts movement around the turn of the century, Gill, Schindler, and the Greenes were interested in designing efficient, well-lit, more sanitary homes that received plenty of fresh air. All believed in straightforward use of basic materials such as wood, stucco, stone, and concrete, as opposed to hiding these beneath assorted period ornamentation, but all treated materials differently. The Greenes were fine wood craftsmen, Schindler was an experimentalist not known for fine detailing, and Gill fell somewhere in between.

All of these architects developed plans that allowed for some interpenetration of indoor and outdoor space, especially Schindler and Gill, and they used progressions of contrasting interior volumes to orchestrate one's emotional experience. But Schindler's sculpting of space was the most progressive. All allowed southern California sites to shape their houses, whether that meant the sprawling Gamble house overlooking the wide-open canyon of the Arroyo Seco, Gill's long, low Dodge house on Kings Road (no longer standing), or Schindler's ground-hugging house just down the street on Kings Road. As mature architects, all philosophically rejected period revival styles in favor of a search for something new and better suited to California. These architects also looked to many different sources of inspiration, near and far. The Greenes drew from India and Japan, Gill from the missions, and Schindler from his Austrian mentors and from old pueblo dwellings of the American Southwest, which he first saw in 1915.

The Greenes are not included in significant discussions of Modern architecture in some well-known books (including ones authored by Nikolaus Pevsner, Charles Jencks, and Kenneth Frampton), probably because of their predominant use of rustic materials such as redwood, brick, stone, and glass, a far cry from the stripped-down, boxy stucco or concrete early Modern houses of Gill, or of Adolf Loos in Vienna. But during their careers, they developed a Modern appreciation of the ways in which buildings can sculpt space and light. While their houses still strike a deep chord with traditionalists, their philosophies were forward-looking.

"The whole Arts and Crafts movement was a stepping stone into Modern architecture," claims Los Angeles architect Randell L. Makinson, who has dedicated a good portion of his career to studying and writing about the Greenes. "I think they were aware that the eclectic past had nothing to do with contemporary society. They embraced logical and rational design determinants, coming from contemporary society, the place, and such elements as available materials and labor force. I suspect there's a great problem about the word Modern. I think that Modernism cannot be hung on a particular period. Maybe a clearer word is contemporary, building in your own time, thinking in your own time."

Fresh out of architecture school at the Massachusetts Institute of Technology, in Boston, the Greenes moved to Pasadena in 1893. With its wide-open spaces and the entrepreneurial spirit of some of its new citizens, Los Angeles was a stimulating place for artists and architects, a place without a cultural past—at least not a traditional European-style past acceptably documented in writing so that traditions could be passed down through generations.

Los Angeles was in the midst of a major transformation from a small settlement to a major urban center. By this time, L.A. was no longer the Wild West, but it still had a pioneering energy. The late 1800s set the stage for an early twentieth-century boom in a city romanticized by real estate, the citrus industry, and health marketing campaigns as an idyllic Arcadia. Between 1870 and 1900, the city's population flourished from 5000 to 100,000, with many of the new arrivals carried west by train after rails connected Los Angeles to Chicago, via San Francisco, in 1869. Dreamers, schemers, movie stars, writers—an optimistic mood of freedom and new possibilities lured hordes of newcomers as Los Angeles grew up, and architects were among them.

Romantic notions of California were enhanced by the national Mission Revival movement that began during the 1890s, spreading homes and public buildings with wavy parapet walls, towers, arches, and tile roofs through the far corners of Los Angeles. The Mission Revival had its own literature. Helen Hunt Jackson's 1884 novel *Ramona* romanticized life on the ranchos in early California and helped spark the Mission Revival. Charles Fletcher Lummis, a Los Angeles writer, promoter, and preservationist, recognized the promotional value of the missions and organized the Landmarks Club in 1894 and 1895 to help preserve missions and use the mission romance to promote southern California.

Into this expansive Mission Revivalist atmosphere came the brothers Greene, who arrived in Pasadena in 1893. Charles Sumner Greene, the older Greene brother, a temperamental, multital-

Gamble House (1908) in Pasadena was one of Greene and Greene's ultimate Craftsman mansions, its low, broad eaves spreading above the gently rounded site.

ented artist with a taste for Emerson and Eastern spirituality, apprenticed in the Boston office of H. Langford Warren, a former associate of Henry Hobson Richardson. Henry Mather Greene, the younger, more practical, steadier Greene brother, apprenticed in Boston with Shepley, Rutan and Coolidge.

Most of the homes designed by the Greenes were on the edges of Pasadena's Arroyo Seco, a wooded valley that inspired their finest Craftsman designs. Here the Greenes developed their own original type of house, characterized by elaborate wood joinery and carving, axial plans that became progressively open and were sometimes arranged around courtyards, cross ventilation, indirect lighting that was progressive for its time, and gently sloping roofs with deep overhanging eaves supported by exposed beam ends.

In an article titled "Architecture on the Pacific Coast," Una Nixson Hopkins applauded the West Coast Craftsman movement, describing "a spontaneity and originality . . . that has grown out of the immediate needs of the people,—who have gathered here from the four corners of the globe,— hence it has no circumscribed creed . . .

"These houses for the most part are of excellent proportions, with sloping roof lines, broad verandas and overhanging eaves . . . The old way of conforming the irregularities of the ground to the building by grading and scraping until an even surface was obtained has been almost entirely abandoned in this new architecture, and in its stead the houses have been designed to conform to the land as nature made it . . .

"The out-of-doors is included in the interior so far as possible—that is, there are a great many doors and windows, and frequently whole rooms of glass . . ."

Hopkins's article ran just as the Greenes hit their prime, and seemed to sum up the Gamble house, one of the brothers' finest homes, completed in 1908. The interior of the Gamble house shows how the brothers were divided between a Modern evolution toward natural light and open interiors and their love of fine wood craftsmanship. For the most part, they extended the Victorian notion of outside and inside as separate space, not closely interconnected, although they did use terraces and sleeping porches closely tied to some rooms. Daylighting at the Gamble house is inconsistent. Some rooms are flooded with natural light, while others take on a shadowy cast due to dark wood paneling that covers many walls. The entry hallway is dim enough that tour guides use flashlights to highlight some of the building's finer wood details.

The interior makes strong ties to the landscape. The entrance consists of a large front door flanked by two smaller doors, the three doors together forming a leaded-glass mural of California live oaks that makes a strong connection with the land. Step inside and you look down a wide central hall that aligns with a pair of rear doors opening to the back garden, providing efficient cross ventilation that was lacking at Schindler's Kings Road house. The Gamble house's attic playroom has operable windows all around that draw warm air up through the central stairway from rooms below and allow it to escape. This movement helps pull in fresh, cooler air through windows and doors on lower floors. The living room is laid out in a cruciform plan, with bays on two sides that reach into the garden, strengthening ties to the landscape.

While all the carved wood speaks of traditional Old World values, the apparent exposure of structural beams, stairway underbellies, and carefully detailed steel bracing seems Modern. In most cases, however, these details were strictly decorative, not structural.

The Greenes are best known for their shingled Pasadena bungalows, but, as Makinson points out, they were not locked into this style, testament to their regionalist approach. In other parts of the state they used materials and forms they never used in southern California. The D. L. James house near Carmel (1918), designed by Charles Greene, is an organic assemblage of stones that seems to grow out of its oceanfront bluff. The Kew house in San Diego (1912) imitated English thatched-roof cottages. The Thomas Gould house in Ventura (1924) was covered with clapboard siding, and the Walter L. Richardson house in Porterville (1929, designed by Henry Greene) was built of adobe bricks.

With Charles's move to an artists colony near Carmel in 1916, the brothers began to drift apart and their practice began to wind down. Their final designs were accomplished during the late 1920s.

During the same time the Greenes were doing their penultimate Craftsman mansions in Pasadena, between 1907 and 1909,

Irving Gill, whose best work was split between San Diego and Los Angeles, was entering his most inventive period in Los Angeles, which lasted from about 1907 until around 1916, when the Dodge house was completed. Gill and the Greenes were contemporaries. Gill was born in Syracuse, New York, in 1870, and Charles and Henry Greene were born in 1868 and 1870, respectively.

After working for Adler and Sullivan in Chicago from 1890 until 1892, Gill moved to San Diego in 1893, the same year the Greenes arrived in Pasadena. Gill's career is treated in more detail in the San Diego section of this book, but his Los Angeles houses deserve mention here.

Gill was a self-taught architect who never attended architecture school. Like the Greenes, his first California work borrowed from East Coast styles, such as the Shingle style, that in turn looked to Europe, and he was also influenced by Frank Lloyd Wright's horizontal, deep-eaved Prairie-style houses.

By 1905, Gill was moving toward his stripped-down interpretation of Mission influences, designing lathe-and-plaster or plaster-covered concrete houses with deep-set window openings and arched breezeways or pergolas that served as transitions between indoors and out. His 1907 Laughlin house in Los Angeles had crisp, smooth lines rendered in concrete and an interior that used less wood than his earlier houses. The 1911 Miltimore house in South Pasadena continued this simple approach, and Gill's 1916 Dodge house in Hollywood (no longer standing), just down the road from Schindler's house, is considered one of Gill's half-dozen finest.

Here was Gill's minimal, flat-roofed concrete aesthetic at its best. The low, large (6500 square feet) house had a courtyard plan that intimately related indoor and outdoor spaces, built-in storage that foreshadowed the Modern Los Angeles houses of the 1930s and 1940s, and 10-foot-high north-facing windows that flooded the main stairwell with natural light.

Between Gill's Los Angeles work of the teens and Schindler's emergence during the twenties, Frank Lloyd Wright began a series of Los Angeles houses that included the concrete block experiments and the Barnsdall house, also known as Hollyhock (1917–20), a mausoleumlike structure

Bare essentials: Gill's 1911 Miltimore house in South Pasadena was a simple cube, softened by pergolas the architect referred to as "green rooms." San Diego Historical Society

Dodge house (1916) was Gill's finest in Los Angeles. The main living areas wrapped around a central patio that made a transition to the expansive garden. Marvin Rand

Elaborately decorated, sometimes overbearing, Wright's Hollyhock house in Hollywood has tightly integrated indoor and outdoor spaces. Sliding doors at the end of the courtyard open the living room wide to the landscape. Sutro

which, despite its ominous presence, makes strong ties to the landscape.

In all, Wright designed twenty-eight concrete block structures, according to Los Angeles historian Robert Sweeney. Of the five that were actually built, three are in L.A., one in Pasadena, all sensitive responses to southern California that made effective use of vastly different sites and were tightly integrated with their landscapes, often designed by Lloyd Wright, Frank's son. The concrete block technology might have had universal potential, but Wright's application was regional.

"In his fifty plus years of designing for California, Wright shifted back and forth between an urge to be regional and a seeming desire to see buildings realized that were variations on themes he had developed for locales all across the country," wrote Gebhard in his 1988 book *California Romanza*. Gebhard felt that Wright "seemed to have generally viewed the whole of coastal southern California as simply an extension of the inland deserts of California and Arizona." Gebhard also observed that in his concrete block houses, Wright drew on primitive Mayan and Aztec architecture— a new way of bringing a Latin flavor to buildings in a state with long Hispanic history. Other architects had looked primarily to the missions and Spanish Colonial architecture for inspiration.

Wright's Millard house (1923) in Pasadena was one of his L.A. concrete block experiments. Sutro

In West Hollywood, Wright's Storer house (1923) nestles comfortably into its hillside. Sutro

Whatever Wright's thinking, he designed several houses in a romantic mode that worked well for southern California. A close look at the Ennis, Millard, and Storer residences, three of the concrete block experiments, shows how carefully he considered their settings. The homes look more wedded to their sites today than when they were completed, since their landscapes have closed in around them. The Ennis house (1924) has large windows and outdoor terraces that link interiors to its lush hillside. The Millard house (1923) dips into an arroyo, on the edge of a pond, with tall windows addressing the view. The Storer house (1923) has tall banks of windows that flood the living room with natural light.

The Sturgis house (1939) was one of Wright's best L.A. houses after the concrete block experiments. Cantilevered daringly over its hillside in Brentwood, the house presents an anonymous face to the street. But behind the blank exterior walls, several glass doors open rooms to a broad deck.

Wright's son, Lloyd, worked on several projects with his father, handling design details and landscape design. While Lloyd Wright's work is nowhere near as well known as his father's, he actually designed many more houses in Los Angeles. The Taggart house in East Hollywood (1922–24) elevated stucco and wood to elegant decorative purpose with a sort of Deco-Egyptian flair. And the Samuels-Navarro house (1926–28) captured a decorative effect similar to his father's earlier concrete block houses, only with pressed metal instead of block.

But it was Schindler who left the most impressive and enduring body of residential work in Los Angeles during the twenties, thirties, and forties, and who seemed divinely inspired by the possibilies of southern California.

"Southern California is a completely unique corner of the United States," Schindler wrote in some notes on Modern architecture he prepared in 1944, on file with the architectural archive at U.C. Santa Barbara. "Although in a tropical latitude, its climate is definitely not tropical. Its flora is neither tropical nor has it real desert characteristics. Its slight seasonal variations lead to a relaxed outdoor life of especial ease. Although its sun is strong, it is controlled by morning fogs. The resulting character of light and color are unique. Instead of the opaque material coloring of the east, we have here the subtle transparent shades created by the light on greyish backgrounds."

Overall, Schindler did not believe American architects were responsive to their regions. In a

Wright's Sturges house (1939) in Brentwood cantilevers dramatically over a steep site. Sutro

Lloyd Wright's Taggart house (1922 to 1924) makes beautiful decorative use of wood and stucco. Sutro

With the Samuels-Navarro house (1926–28), Lloyd Wright used pressed metal to achieve a decorative effect reminiscent of his father's concrete block houses. Julius Shulman

letter to Neutra in late 1920 or early 1921, Schindler wrote: "The only buildings which testify to the deep feeling for the soil on which they stand are the sunbaked adobe buildings of the firsts immigrants and their successors—Spanish and American—in the southwestern part of the country." His appreciation of these vernacular structures is visible in his earliest buildings, including the Kings Road house, with its comfortable but spare interiors enclosed by simple solid walls.

An essential shift in American society helped shape Schindler's houses. Whereas the Greenes and Gill included servants' quarters in many of their plans, Schindler designed houses for servantless clients. With affordable land in Los Angeles and a new prosperous middle class emerging during the thirties and forties, wealthy people were no longer the only ones who could hire architects to design their homes.

Schindler didn't buy into the "International Style" of Modernism, a term invented by Phillip Johnson and Henry-Russell Hitchcock for a show they organized and held at the Museum of Modern Art in New York in 1932. Instead of the International Style's emphasis on functional and formal use of new structural technology, Schindler was interested in "the creation of space forms—dealing with a new medium as rich and unlimited in possibilities of expression as any other media of art: color, sound, mass, etc.," he wrote in his essay "Space Architecture," first published in 1934 in *Dune Forum* magazine.

"The essential characteristic of the machine is its capacity for exact repetition—its effort is one-dimensional," he added in a 1936 article, "Furniture and the Modern House," published in *Architect and Engineer* in 1935 and 1936.

"Yet the essence of life is variation. In direct contrast with the limited power of a machine. The house which helps articulate us must allow further variation. It must be four-dimensional . . .

"The house of the future is a symphony of 'space forms'—each room a necessary and unavoidable part of the whole. Structural materials, walls, ceilings, floors, are only means to an end: the definition of space forms."

And, again in "Space Architecture," Schindler differentiated himself from such Modern architects as the Frenchman Le Corbusier:

"Most of the buildings which Corbusier and his followers offer us as 'machines to live in,' equipped with various 'machines to sit and sleep on,' have not even reached the state of development of our present machines. They are crude 'contraptions' to serve a purpose. The man who brings such machines into his living room is on the same level of primitive development as the farmer who keeps cows and pigs in his house."

Schindler was born in Vienna in 1887 and entered architecture, with Otto Wagner and Adolf Loos as mentors, at a time when Austrian intellectuals such as Freud and Wittgenstein were in their prime. Even before he came to the United States, Schindler was very familiar with Wright's work. He arrived in New York in 1914 and worked for OSR in Chicago from 1914 through 1917, then began an intermittent six-year stint working for Wright that included a significant role in the design and construction supervision of Wright's Hollyhock House in Los Angeles, a job that brought Schindler to the city in the first place.

Schindler's own houses show a sensitivity not only to the Los Angeles as a whole, but to distinctive micro-regions. In Wrightian fashion, their designs grow out of the contours of different sites; interior plans and spatial organization strengthen ties between the houses and the landscape.

His Kings Road house is long and low, following the wide-open lay of what was then undeveloped land, while his Lovell house at Newport Beach, with its five massive concrete frames, is oriented toward ocean views and elevated on concrete piers that echo nearby ocean piers, so that the "ground floor" is a usable sandy beach. His houses mostly fell into two categories: early single-story places, and the hillside houses of the thirties and forties.

While Schindler rejected some facets of Modernism, he was interested in efficiency through the use of a standard module, although he wasn't revolutionary in this thinking and didn't use repeated modular forms and dimensions with consistency. Some of his houses, including the one on Kings Road, used 4-foot spacing for structural members.

Schindler also explored the idea of prefabricated parts that could be transported to a site and quickly assembled into a house. In 1931, he proposed what he called a "Schindler Shelter," a house of modular parts that he said could be built for less than $3000 at a time when an average family home cost $6000 to $7000.

There's a longstanding debate about the importance of Schindler, the artist-architect who was never popular during his career, versus his onetime friend and peer Neutra, who, through his flair for getting designs published and exhibited, achieved international acclaim. Regardless of what you think of either, they were the two most influential architects of their generation in Los Angeles.

Early pictures show two men of strikingly different appearance. Neutra was tall, slim, pale, and often wore a tie. Schindler was 5' 7", heavier set, often tan, and preferred to dress in loose-fitting silk shirts he had custom made. Late in his career, during the 1940s, when writer Esther McCoy worked for him, he drove from job site to job site in a car from which he had removed the backseat to make room for his dog and building supplies, according to her book *Five California Architects*. Wood was often tied to the top, and the trunk might be full of "sheet metal parts, cans of paint and caulking compound and a complete set of tools."

Schindler and Neutra met in Vienna around 1912, where they were drawn to Austrian architects Otto Wagner and Adolf Loos as early role models, and they shared a desire to come to America, fueled by their enthusiasm for Frank Lloyd Wright's work. Wright's building designs were first seen by many Europeans in 1910 in a publication known as the Wasmuth portfolio. Schindler came to America in 1914, Neutra, who was five years younger, in 1925. Schindler arrived in Los Angeles in 1920 to supervise construction of Wright's Barnsdall house; Neutra and his wife came to live with the Schindlers at Kings Road in 1926.

Schindler and Neutra were good friends in Austria and for their first years in Los Angeles, but their friendship chilled in 1930 after Neutra toured Europe showing drawings for a joint project without using Schindler's name. The split widened as Neutra became internationally known and Schindler remained relatively obscure. Neutra's designs were included in the 1932 International Style show, Schindler's were not.

According to McCoy's 1960 book *Richard Neutra*, Neutra appreciated the new technology of the Modern machine age, but also had an organic side stemming from his interest in biological sciences. This came out not in the site-sensitive planning and flowing interior spaces of Wright and Schindler, but in Neutra's dedication to the idea that architects must understand the human organism in order to design the best possible buildings. For Neutra, this meant precise, machinelike houses of steel and glass, but Schindler didn't believe in the International Style's cool aesthetic. He didn't feel this was suitable for Los Angeles.

"Functionalism with its white stucco, stainless steel, glass and poster color schemes is here more out of place than anywhere else on this continent," he wrote in 1944 in unpublished personal notes on Modern architecture, on file at U.C. Santa Barbara. "The attempt to root the building in this extraordinary soil is confined to a few (Schindler, Ain, Lind . . .)."

Neutra's plans were open but generally more rigid than Schindler's, which had the drama associated with Wright's designs. Schindler clustered rooms so that space would flow through a house, and his plans seem inspired more by emotion than rigid geometric logic. While both Schindler and Neutra innovated with materials ranging from steel and concrete to plywood, the experiments of each left different impressions.

Houses designed by Schindler and Neutra for the same client, Dr. Philip Lovell, illustrate essential differences between their approaches. Lovell

Schindler's Lovell beach house (1926) is supported by five concrete frames, elevated above Newport Beach like a lifeguard tower or pier. Julius Shulman

wrote a syndicated column on health and homeopathic medicine for the *Los Angeles Times*, and both Schindler and Neutra's houses responded to his desire for a healthy, outdoors-oriented lifestyle. Schindler's Newport Beach house for Lovell was completed in 1926, Neutra's hillside Lovell house in East Hollywood in 1929.

Schindler's Lovell house has many layers of formal and spatial complexity. The design is a direct response to the site, derived in part from pier structures and lifeguard towers found in beach communities, elevated above the sand for protection and to enhance ocean views. The house rests on concrete piers, leaving the bottom level open as a usable beach/backyard, with the extra height contributing to privacy on the upper levels.

Structurally, the house was revolutionary. Five parallel concrete frames support the building, with wood joists between them holding up floors, and walls of metal lathe and cement plaster suspended from the frames. An open balcony was intended as sleeping space, and there was a rooftop deck for sunbathing. The beach-facing side of the house

Neutra's Lovell house (1929) pioneered the use of steel framing, carried on later by Raphael Soriano and Pierre Koenig.
Julius Shulman

The open, transparent Kaufman house (1948) was Neutra's sensitive response to the Palm Springs desert and showed his commitment to integrating his architecture with the landscapes he designed. Julius Shulman

features bold, projecting forms set into sharp relief by spaces and recesses, including the long horizontal strip of the top-level deck.

Neutra's Lovell house shows his fascination with the application of industrial steel framing to residential construction, dating back to his work with Holabird and Roche, Chicago architects who designed large steel-frame buildings, mainly hotels. Neutra photographed several steel buildings under construction in Chicago in 1924. The Lovell house's steel frame was welded in sections and trucked to the site, where it was assembled in forty hours. Thin walls are of concrete sprayed over metal forms.

After living in both houses, Lovell did not find the house Neutra designed for him nearly as hospitable as Schindler's.

"It had no lilt, no happiness, no joy," he told Esther McCoy for her 1979 book *Vienna to Los Angeles: Two Journeys.* "It was a public museum. And it got to be an albatross.

"It was a serious, dignified house but I didn't belong there. The plan was too Germanic—the children and housekeeper getting the worst, their rooms on the north were cold, and the master getting the best, all the sun. No possibility for nude sunbathing. No possibility for sleeping in the open (actually, plans showed three sleeping porches, but Lovell apparently found these too narrow). We screened in a porch to sleep on but the beds

were twelve inches apart. He (Neutra) called it Health House but RMS (Schindler) gave us more along those lines."

In later years, Neutra continued to explore the possibilities of steel and glass with houses that, superficially, looked similar to each other, while Schindler's houses were more diverse and often more tied to their locales through the materials he selected.

Neutra's famous Kaufman house in Palm Springs (1948) was in the same language as the houses he was doing in Los Angeles at the time: huge expanses of glass, tall ceilings, steel frame, an early Case Study approach. By contrast, Schindler's Toole house in Palm Springs (1946) was a desert variant on wood and/or stucco houses that dominated his Los Angeles residential work of this period. The desert house incorporated walls of stone that anchored the building to the desert.

Over the years, Neutra stayed with basic rectilinear forms, but he eventually experimented with wood for both structure and sheathing, and even built the Nesbitt house (1942) of wood and brick. Increasingly during the 1940s, Neutra used earlier experience he gained working as a landscape architect in Switzerland to offset his rectilinear plans with curvilinear landscapes and water features. Some of his late forties and fifties houses step into the landscape with outrigger structural "legs" of steel or wood.

Neutra's house for East Coast radio commentator John Nesbitt (1942) had such high ceilings and open interiors that it prompted Nesbitt to marvel "It's so big!" when he first saw it, according to photographer Julius Shulman. Julius Shulman

The dining room at Davidson's own house (1948) merged with the garden through a floor-to-ceiling opening. Julius Shulman

Meanwhile, as Schindler evolved, his architecture grew more complex and varied. Following his twenties experiments with concrete, including his own house and the Lovell house, Schindler faced the reality of lower Depression-era budgets and built with wood frame and plaster.

He sheathed some houses in wood, and used stone for some walls. His forties residential designs were marked by variations in roof types, but not for the sake of style or appearance. In his 1971 book *Schindler*, Gebhard explains that Schindler "employed a shed or gable roof as a solution to the problem of vertical space internally, not for its picturesque qualities externally."

While Neutra achieved early acclaim, Schindler came to be appreciated over time, as even his early critics changed their opinions. After Schindler died in 1953, Phillip Johnson, who had given Schindler short shrift while organizing the 1932 International Style show, eulogized Schindler in *California Arts + Architecture* magazine as "among the great pioneers of modern architecture in this country." And in an introduction to Gebhard's book on Schindler, Hitchcock admitted that he, too, had midjudged Schindler when, in 1932, he wrote:

"The case of Schindler I do not profess to understand. There is certainly immense vitality, perhaps somewhat lacking among many of the best architects of the Pacific Coast. But this vitality seems in general to lead to arbitrary and brutal effects . . . Schindler's manner does not seem to mature. His continued reflection of the somewhat hectic psychological air of the region, from which all the others have attempted to protect themselves, still produces something of the look of sets for a Wellesian 'film of the future.'"

But by the time he wrote the preface for Gebhard's book, Hitchcock had transformed his earlier opinion, seeming to realize his early naivete as an Easterner giving an uninformed, knee-jerk reaction to Schindler's work.

"Happily, Mr. Gebhard knows well the southern California scene: thus he is able to place Schindler's work in relation to its specific American milieu and thereby, perhaps, to propose a significant, if not a full, appreciation of those aspects of Schindler's work that once found so little acceptance from critics of the East Seaboard such as myself. I am glad that this Foreward gives me an opportunity to make some redress for the narrow-minded approach to Schindler, and indeed to modern architecture in California more generally, of a generation ago."

Other architects were emerging during the 1930s, several of whom were European and had ties to Neutra or Schindler.

In 1923, J. R. Davidson came to New York from Berlin, and the following year moved to Los

Angeles, where he became friends with Kem Weber (another transplanted Berliner), Neutra, and Schindler. Weber came to San Francisco in 1914 to help design the German portion of the Panama-Pacific Exposition in San Francisco and moved to Los Angeles in 1921, where he eventually became a leading proponent of the popular Art Deco style known as Streamline Moderne.

Gregory Ain met Neutra and Schindler early in his development as an architect, and apprenticed with Neutra, who encouraged budding architects to learn architecture by working in his office instead of going to architecture school. In 1930, Ain was among several young architects, including Harwell Hamilton Harris, who came together under Neutra as a new Los Angeles chapter of CIAM (Congres Internationaux d'Architecture Moderne) to prepare projects to be presented by Neutra at CIAM's 1930 conference in Brussels. Harris was bound for architecture school at U.C. Berkeley in 1928, but spent the summer working for Neutra and never made it to college. Instead, he soon found himself working on drawings for Neutra's Lovell house.

Raphael Soriano was born on the Greek island of Rhodes, and, like Ain, studied architecture at U.S.C. once he arrived in Los Angeles. Soriano worked for Neutra in the summer of 1932, later worked briefly for Schindler, then again for Neutra. Craig Ellwood and Pierre Koenig worked for Soriano and continued his steel-frame explorations.

The University of Southern California was influential from the thirties through the fifties, bringing many of these architects together. U.S.C. alums included Soriano, Koenig, Harris, and Ellwood. But U.S.C. wasn't open to all types of architecture, as Esther McCoy noted in *Vienna to Los Angeles*: "The staid USC School of Architecture wanted no part of Wright, Schindler or Neutra."

Beginning in the late thirties, Soriano spent more than twenty years perfecting the use of lightweight steel in residential designs, before turning to other framing materials including aluminum. His houses sometimes incorporated Neutra's strip windows, smooth stucco walls, and flat roofs; like Neutra, Soriano sometimes

The steel frame of Soriano's Curtis house (1950) shows how free and open an interior could be with his progressive structural system. Julius Shulman

went so far as to paint wood to match the metal on his houses. Unlike some of the other architects then using steel frames, Soriano usually concealed his behind plaster, rather than expressing it. Also unlike some steel-framers, Soriano used color in his designs, including yellows, greens, and blues.

Due to its steel frame, Soriano's 1950 Curtis residence needed no interior load-bearing walls, which allowed an extremely open interior. With the Curtis house, he also employed factory-built storage wall partitions containing closets, drawers, shelving, counters, and storage, to divide the house into rooms. In subsequent years, Soriano repeated his modular means of building, with results that met a range of client needs and produced a variety of spaces and moods, proving that an industrial approach to home building could achieve individuality and warmth. Soriano came close to translating his methods to the masses when he designed a home for tract builder Joseph Eichler in Palo Alto in 1955, but Eichler decided not to try steel in his tracts.

Unlike many of the well-known L.A. architects of the thirties and forties, who came from Europe, Harwell Hamilton Harris was a third generation Californian born in Redlands, near San Bernardino. Harris started out as sculp-

Ain was among the first of the L.A. Modernists to experiment with hipped roofs, as on the Daniel house (1939), to make his interiors more spacious and varied. Julius Shulman

A glass wall and vine-covered trellis help merge the interior of the Daniel house with the surrounding landscape. Julius Shulman

tor, but told Esther McCoy for her book *The Second Generation* that seeing Frank Lloyd Wright's Hollyhock house sparked his interest in becoming an architect. He was accepted into the architecture school at U.C. Berkeley, but instead took a job with Neutra producing drawings for the Lovell house.

For Harris's first solo house design, he wanted to use Bubblestone, a foamy liquid material not intended for residential construction, into which fabric such as burlap was dipped then laid over the frame of the house to harden. But Harris could not get bank financing. Nor could he get financing for a flat-roofed house with walls of plywood panels with an aluminum foil core. He ended up using redwood siding and a hipped roof, configuring the house in an L shape around a garden, with two bedrooms and the living room oriented toward their own outdoor gardens and terrace.

Harris's wood-and-glass pavilion in Fellowship Park (1935) in Los Angeles, wide open to the canyon view, was one of his best- known designs. In its simplicity, fiber-mat flooring, and strong relationship to the landscape, it made an impression reminiscent of a Japanese teahouse.

Harris's work proved popular with design journals and with his peers. In *The Second Generation*, McCoy explains that "professional magazines saw Harris as a gifted designer in the Bay Region style . . . Los Angeles critics saw Harris as someone who

bridged the years between Greene and Greene and the 1930s, using wood more directly and economically, but with grace and elegant detailing."

Gregory Ain, who launched his career with several years in Neutra's office and opened his own office in 1935, took a socialist approach to architecture and was as well known for his multifamily plans as for single-family homes. He experimented with various prefabricated units such as walls and bathrooms to keep costs down.

"There was nothing clever or intricate about Ain's designs," McCoy wrote in *The Second Generation*. "His houses presented no sudden surprises, nothing underscaled or overscaled to delight or confound the eye; none of Schindler's sharp wit . . ."

After some thirties flat-roofed houses that shared Schindler's fascination with asymmetrical assemblages of rectilinear forms that gained energy from recesses, cutouts, and projecting eaves, Ain used shed, hipped, and other roof forms in the forties. Ain often used high clerestory strips to daylight a room while retaining privacy, and, like Schindler, he sometimes wrapped corners in glass to gain daylighting and to help interiors merge with the landscape.

The Eames house and studio (1947–49), designed by Charles Eames, proved that industrial steel framing could produce inviting residential space. It was one of the earliest and most significant Case Study Houses Julius Shulman

Rhythms of solid and void, light and shadow, make the Eames house a living, changing sculpture.   Julius Shulman

A mong L.A.'s architectural schools, U.S.C. made a significant contribution by serving as a focus for the Case Study Houses program, which was founded by John Entenza while he was editor of *Arts and Architecture* magazine from 1945 to 1962. Koenig, Soriano, A. Quincy Jones, Whitney Smith, and several other Case Study architects studied architecture and/or taught at U.S.C.

Entenza wanted to explore ways of building prototypical small houses for the servantless middle class, with the idea that these designs could eventually become affordable through the use of mass-produced modular parts. The program began as World War II ended and construction of new housing was expected to take off to meet pent-up demand left over from the Depression era.

Davidson, Neutra, Charles Eames, and Michigan-based architect Eero Saarinen, designed the first Case Study Houses. Later, young architects such as Koenig and Ellwood, both former draftsmen for Soriano, boosted their careers by designing Case Studies of their own.

According to Esther McCoy, houses by Charles Eames, an industrial designer, and Saarinen (with Eames) were the most experimental in plan and structure, also the first to utilize industrial materials.

The Eames house in Pacific Palisades has become one of the most famous Los Angeles houses, proving that a boxy steel frame can define lively, inviting spaces.

As Eames commented in Esther McCoy's 1977 book *Case Study Houses*, ". . . it is interesting to consider how the rigidity of the system was responsible for the free use of space and to see how the most

Koenig's Case Study #21 (1958) used steel post-and-beam to cantilever the living room dramatically over its Hollywood hillside. Julius Shulman

Ellwood's Rose residence (1962) was a steel, brick, and glass pavilion, radical in its deliberate separation of house from landscape. Julius Shulman

matter-of-fact structure resulted in pattern and texture." By incorporating stucco panels of white, blue, red, black, and earth tones with clear and opaque glass, Eames gave the house a more complex, intriguing appearance than other steel-frame houses.

In the fifties and sixties, Ellwood, Soriano, and Pierre Koenig were among Case Study architects who dedicated themselves to further exploring the possibilities of steel-frame construction for houses, extending a line of steel experimentation begun in Los Angeles during the twenties by Neutra.

Joh n Lautner was a loner outside the group of Los Angeles architects who descended from Neutra or Schindler, or who worked on the Case Studies.

Lautner apprenticed in architecture at Taliesin, Frank Lloyd Wright's hands-on architecture school in Arizona and Wisconsin, where Lautner spent six years during the 1930s. His first house on his own was a "calling card" place for himself in 1940.

Largely bypassed by critical or popular acclaim, Lautner is in his eighties now and still designing houses. Like Wright or Buckminster Fuller, he is part sci-fi futurist, part design genius. Chemosphere, the flying-saucer-like house he designed in 1960 in Hollywood, now looks like a period piece out of *Popular Mechanics*, but other Lautner houses have a timeless appeal. Rainbow Top (1962) is marvelously transparent and has a sweeping roofline that mimics the soft curve of its site. A house in Malibu (1979) is framed with sweeping wood lam beams and has a broad

Chemosphere (1960) was Lautner's means of gaining integrated living space on a steep hillside lot. Julius Shulman

This infrared photo dramatizes the sweeping view from inside Chemosphere. Julius Shulman

Lautner's "Rainbow Top" house (1962) has a sweeping roof that marries the house to the soft curve of its site. Julius Shulman

A master of defining space, Lautner used architecture to lead the eye toward the ocean with this house in Malibu (1979). Julius Shulman

expanse of glass panels butted together to frame a panoramic ocean view.

As an educator, Los Angeles architect Ray Kappe played a significant role in the emergence of much of the experimental architecture of the 1970s and 1980s. Kappe attended architecture school at Cal Berkeley, where William Wurster became dean during Kappe's last year, 1951.

During the fifties in Los Angeles, Kappe aligned himself with such architects as Whitney Smith and Calvin Straub, both U.S.C. graduates and lecturers. Kappe, Smith, Straub, and other architects were building wood post-and-beam houses, houses Kappe considered to be "our extension of Harwell Harris's integration of Greene and Greene and Wright and Neutra. I think people felt there was a regional attitude around southern California. It may have just been a lot of architects working in a similar vein, but most of us thought we were bringing forward Modern traditions from Greene and Greene.

"Southern California has this good climate, which gives you the ability to open houses up and move them into the landscape.

Kappe's own post-and-beam house (1968) was built on six concrete pads to minimize grading and has living platforms connected by bridges and stairs, merged with the landscape through abundant glass. Julius Shulman

"The problem that goes on as you get further into it is, you can also make a case for regionalism related to what is going on in the streets, in different parts of the city. When we were doing it, it was hills and view sites. Now, you can make a case for Frank Gehry and so forth as a regional aspect of L.A."

Kappe was an essential link between the 1950s and 1960s and the experimental L.A. architects of the seventies and eighties, not stylistically but through his involvement with education. Kappe chaired the first architecture department at Cal Poly Pomona near Los Angeles from 1968 until 1972. Following disagreements with the school adminstration, he left in 1972 with about fifty students and instructors including Jim Stafford and Thom Mayne to start a new architecture school called the Southern California Institute of Architecture, or Sci-Arc. Eric Owen Moss joined the faculty two years later.

One of Kappe's reasons for leaving was that he wanted students to be more involved with the education process, rather than being spoon-fed information in a rigid academic setting. Sci-Arc has developed a reputation as a scrappy, hands-on school that pushes students to think independantly, to come up with original design solutions.

Sci-Arc's orientation during the mid-seventies was toward technology, the environment, and social issues, Kappe recalls. But with architects such as Aldo Rossi, Charles Moore (who taught at U.C.L.A. during the late 1970s), Michael Graves, and Robert Stern making anti-Modern waves during the late seventies and early eighties, rejecting rigid, austere Modernism in favor of color, decoration, texture, and borrowed historical forms, the designs of students and faculty at Sci-Arc also headed in new directions.

As a student at Sci-Arc, Michael Rotondi met Mayne, an instructor, and the two went on to become partners in Morphosis beginning in 1976. The firm became one of the most influential in L.A. during the eighties. Gehry taught at Sci-Arc for a term during the late seventies.

As Kappe hinted when explaining his generation's brand of regionalism, the generation that came next also responded to Los Angeles, but instead of designing for pristine hillside sites with views, they were often building in tight urban set-

Late Case Study? Rediscovered Wright? No. Gehry, working in a classic L.A. post-and-beam style with the Steves residence (1959) years before he emerged as the quintessential artist-architect. Julius Shulman

Gehry remodeled his own house (1978) by wrapping it in corrugated metal and chain-link fencing, signaling the start of a new era in L.A. architecture and shocking several neighbors Tim Street-Porter

tings, sometimes using utilitarian materials found in these surroundings. Their choice of materials was also dictated by limited client budgets. The young L.A. architects of the seventies and eighties also brought new humor to their architecture. Most were quite serious about their designs, but some also believed a house should provoke smiles or chuckles, such as when Gehry created amusing dialogues between his old house and the addition

he made, or Brian Murphy used shattered glass stair treads.

Gehry signaled a new movement with a 1978 remodel of his house in Santa Monica, wrapping the steep-roofed thirties Dutch Colonial with an addition of corrugated metal, chain-link fencing, and exposed timbering, leaving portions of the old house intact within the new outer walls. You can walk through the new front door, then through the old front door behind it. Gehry bared portions of the old wood frame inside, and blew out ceilings to open spaces to the rafters. Gehry's violations of traditional rules of construction, such as running beams through window openings, baring wood frames, and eliminating usual boundaries between rooms, showed his emerging conception of architecture as sculpture as much as utilitarian container for living. Often Gehry designs houses as clusters of interrelated pieces scattered in a landscape, as with his Schnabel residence, included here. With smaller volumes, he can give each room a more intimate scale as well as better natural light and crossventilation.

Fred Fisher, a Gehry alum included in this book, left Gehry's office in 1980 to design his first house on his own. Fisher acknowledges his connection to Gehry, both in the ways Gehry elevated the status of low-brow materials such as chain-link fence and corrugated metal, and in Gehry's philosophic approach.

"I went to a lecture by him when I was in grad school at U.C.L.A.," Fisher says. "I had seen his work published before, but the way he thought about things was very special, the strong component of referring to art and the art process. That really struck a chord with me that was coincident with my own interests."

Early houses by Fisher show Gehry's influence in their materials, sculptural forms, and exposed structure, but more recent houses such as the Bleifer residence, included in this book, take a more restrained approach and benefit from higher budgets that allow higher quality materials. Fisher still takes an artistic approach. He speaks of "collaging" and "mixing and matching" of seemingly disparate elements.

Moss's Petal House, completed near Westwood in 1983, became famous through worldwide publication. Editors seemed to perceive it as the far-out

Petals open to the sky around a rooftop hot tub. Moss's "Petal House" (1983) was a spirited response to life in southern California. Tim Street-Porter

Murphy's home for Dennis Hopper in Venice presents a stark corrugated steel face to its gritty neighborhood. Sutro

epitome of Los Angeles residential design, an asphalt-shingled addition to a forties tract bungalow, crowned by four petallike triangular walls that enclose a rooftop deck and hot tub. Instead of wrapping the old structure inside the new, as Gehry did with his own house, Moss left the original intact and added on top of it. Like Gehry and Fisher, Moss has a love of cheap chic materials, such as asphalt-shingle roofing used to sheath walls, steel rebar as a front porch screen and security barrier, and corrugated metal, and he likes to expose wood framing, especially to emphasize transitions between old and new or between various forms and spaces.

Rotondi, who is dean of Sci-Arc today, and Mayne produced several interesting houses together before Rotondi left Morphosis in 1991 to explore new directions that include collaboration with artists from other disciplines and computers as a tool for expanding his design consciousness. The Venice "alley houses" designed by Morphosis during the 1980s used asphalt shingle, concrete block, corrugated metal roofing and siding, which made them cousins of Fisher, Gehry, and Moss's work, but Mayne and Rotondi's penchant for meticulous detailing and rigorous plans has earned them the respect of such predecessors as Kappe, one of their mentors at Sci-Arc.

Many of these architects elevate low-brow materials from industrial to residential use, and sometimes the materials speak of the strained social climate in Los Angeles, especially where architects are designing for urban sites in tough neighborhoods.

Brian Murphy's Venice home for actor Dennis Hopper addresses the street with a forbidding wall of corrugated metal, with all the color, light, and action reserved for inside, and his Dixon residence in a rundown Venice neighborhood has covered over windows and an address graffitied on a scarred stucco wall—the impression from the street is of an abandoned house no one would mess with. Again, the interior gets all the action. In tight urban settings, where security is a concern and there is no space for a garden, these younger architects have been forced to establish different indoor/outdoor relationships than Schindler and Gill were able to accomplish on large flat sites or secluded hillside lots.

Murphy, who dropped out of graduate school in architecture at U.C.L.A. and opened his practice in 1982, shares his contemporaries' dedication to straightforward use of basic materials such as wood and steel, and to sculptural forms and daylight-flooded interiors, but he adds his own unusual sensibility to interiors furnished with found objects: doorknobs as faucets, grass skirts transformed into sconces, clip-on photographers' lamps combined into a chandelier.

Like Gehry, who admits he has one foot in art, one in architecture, Murphy is influenced by what's happening in other media, as when he saw the movie *Dangerous Liaisons*, set in the eighteenth century, and decided to design a house lit with candles. Murphy, a skilled carpenter, is unusual in the degree of control he exerts over projects, functioning not only as architect but as landscape and interior designer and contractor.

And now a new generation is emerging. Although many of the young L.A. architects look to Gehry, to the dynamic, socially troubled Los Angeles of today, to art, to technology, and to other contemporary phenomena for inspiration, there is also, among many of them, a sense of connection to the past. For some of these architects, Schindler has been an irresistible icon.

"Neutra has been a hero for many years. Schindler has been ignored, when in some respects he was probably better," says Hank Koning, whose own house, included in this book and designed in collaboration with his wife, Julie, tempers Schindler's fascination with indoor/outdoor connections, expressed structure, and bare concrete with a lean geometric logic seldom found in Schindler's work.

Schweitzer, whose own desert home is included here, also acknowledges Schindler as an influence. Schindler never used wild colors like Schweitzer does, but Schindler's houses of the thirties and forties, with their stacked and colliding forms, share a geometric tension with Schweitzer's. His desert house is a series of cubes, with trapezoidal window and door openings that jangle the underlying order.

In a way that now seems amazingly prescient given architects such as Gehry, Moss, and Morphosis, Schindler pushed against the boundaries of what could be done with materials and construction methods, but he was most concerned with making great spaces. He combined forms into kinetic architectural sculptures which, as architectural historian David Gebhard has noted, sometimes had parallels in the de Stijl and other art movements, and which captured the energy of a densifying, increasingly complex city. Schindler's houses cannot be grasped in terms of a single conceptual idea, but instead push you toward an acceptance of contradiction and complexity as valid results, foreshadowing architects such as Gehry, Moss, and Rotondi. As Rotondi has written since he left Morphosis, an essential task faced by today's L.A. architects is to find means of architectural expression that will help reconcile the city's diverse social forces, which will continue colliding and interacting as the city careens toward the turn of the century.

Gehry made the Schnabel residence (1989) intimate by breaking it into several distinct elements. The copper dome atop the guest unit was inspired by the dome of Griffith Park Observatory. Sutro

Los Angeles is a city of contradictions, a chaotic metropolis surrounded by placid ocean, mountains, and deserts. Architect Frank Israel addressed these extremes of urban grit and elemental beauty with a house for Hollywood talent agent Howard Goldberg and real estate agent Jim Bean.

The Goldberg-Bean residence occupies a sweeping corner on a dramatic view site in the Hollywood Hills, and its rooms align with the street grids of three urban areas, all visible from the house: downtown L.A. (the entrance gallery), Hollywood (the living room), and Santa Monica (the master suite).

The street wall encloses a protected entry court, a decompression zone that eases visitors toward the door. Stucco in earthy tones is the "glue" that visually pulls together disparate materials such as wood, steel, frosted glass, stainless steel, and concrete block. Tom Bonner

A cobalt-blue plaster wall ties living areas together. Walls neatly meet floors and ceilings without moldings, a finicky Israel-ian detail that drives workers crazy. A gridded window wall pays homage to R. M. Schindler, one of Israel's heroes. Tom Bonner

Dusky glow descends on the house after sunset as the translucent steel-and-frosted-glass awning filters changing colors of the sky and the stainless steel front door swings open to a wide entry hall and views of the garden and downtown L.A. David Glomb

Israel selected a cherry wood living room floor with a dark stain, because "I was tired of all those light oak floors." Tom Bonner

Steel structural beams double as posts that stake out the master bed. Lam beams run through the bedroom and adjacent master closet, supporting a second-level office and deck. Tom Bonner

Counter to this Cartesian order, the interior of the house is meant to suggest natural themes of fire (fireplaces), air (dramatic openings), and water (the pool and spacious master shower). Israel hopes this elemental grounding "gives the participants a sense of removal from what is seemingly hostile and rude about urban life."

The house is a series of pavilions joined on the inside by a serpentine cobalt-blue wall. The wall strings together a master suite/office tower, expansive central living space, and a guest wing. All of these spaces have open visual and circulation ties to the garden. Plants brush up against windows along the back of the house, and wide sliding glass doors open the central space to the landscape.

Dynamic forms grew out of functional requirements. Columns support the second-story office and double as posts that stake out the canopied master bed. Meaty structural lam beams punch dramatically through the master closet and bedroom and extend outside to hold up a deck.

Like some of his Los Angeles peers, Israel puts basic materials to imaginative use. A sail-like awning of steel and frosted glass flies over the entry, and the floor just inside is polished concrete aggregate with inlaid strips of stainless steel. Lead-coated copper panels cover the back wall of the master suite, which bulges like an airplane fuselage, and the second-level studio office above the suite is covered with fir plywood and redwood battens. Stucco in mustard yel-

Lead-coated copper panels cover the bowed back of the master suite, which supports a second-story office covered with fir plywood and redwood battens.
Tom Bonner

At dusk, the master suite glows from within like a Japanese lantern. David Glomb

low and orangy red, and the red clay tile roof, add stabilizing, earthy weight to the exterior.

Schooled at the University of Pennsylvania during architect Louis Kahn's reign, based in Los Angeles, Israel, forty-seven, has an increasingly clear vision of what he wants to accomplish with his buildings. It's an agenda that includes responding imaginatively to each site, designing architecture that is relevant to a complex society on the brink of a new century, and creating buildings that will last.

"I think Schindler was the most talented and creative architect in California," Israel says of his favorite early California Modernist. "Buildings by Schindler, Neutra, and Wright were very experimental, and because of relatively primitive building technology became an easy target of criticism when they didn't hold up."

With the Goldberg-Bean house, Israel balances free use of colors, forms, and materials with meticulous Craftsmanship that proves progressive new architecture can seem permanent.

Los Angeles architect Brian Murphy is not averse to wild color in his designs, but a client with a hankering for cool monochrome prompted this spare, minimalist house that relies on subtle variations of light, shadow, and texture to achieve high drama.

Situated on a prime lot in the Hollywood Hills, the house is actually a remodel of a place that had already been remodeled several times, leaving a mess that Murphy says resembled two double-wide mobile homes. He kept the L-shaped footprint and kidney pool and organized the extensive makeover around a vaulted central living space that slashes through the corner of the *L* on a diagonal, aligned with the spectacular view to downtown.

Spacious and open, the interior has few rooms: The master suite and kitchen flank the new central space, with its separate glassed-in music room and second-level catwalk accessing a wall of books. On clear winter days when wind and rain cleanse away smog, the L.A. skyline is visible, beyond the pool, through a bank of steel-sash windows at the end of the vaulted central space.

Murphy prefers creative use of stock materials to exotic stone or expensive designer fixtures.

"I've spent a lot of time in Mexico, surfing off the coast,

Clients requested monochrome, so Murphy played basic volumes off each other and wrapped them in basic materials such as white corrugated fiberglass and white wood clapboards. William Mount

Past the pond, under the steel-mesh deck, is the modest front door, which gives no hint of the soaring space just inside. During rainstorms, water rushes down chain "gutter." William Mount

White predominates, serving as a backdrop for subtle plays of light and shadow. The edge of the kitchen looks past the corner of the view-facing window wall into the living room. William Mount

Murphy tied the house together with a grand vaulted central space, aimed at the downtown L.A. skyline. Beneath the catwalk library, first-floor glass doors lead to separate music room. William Mount

A serious cooks' kitchen has triangular prep islands on wheels and double doors that open to the entry court. William Mount

A stainless-steel mixing bowl became a basin in the powder room, a glass shower cube has custom hardware assembled from stock fittings and lengths of copper pipe. Walls, floor, and ceiling are white tile. William Mount

The sun reaches deep into the house during winter through the south-facing window wall, casting a shadowy grid. A wide hall connects central living spaces with the master bedroom. William Mount

and if something breaks down there, you make do with what you've got," says Murphy, who grew up in southern California. "A lot of people send off to Italy for exotic stuff, and I think it's ridiculous."

He covered the garage, the most visible part of the house, with corrugated fiberglass, and gave it a metal roof that sweeps up on two corners. At night, this translucent cube glows like the world's largest Japanese lantern, and Murphy claims police helicopters use it for navigation. A powder room features a square glass shower stall with a pool light aimed up from the white tile floor, and a stainless steel mixing bowl adapted as a sink.

New steel columns freed the master suite of load-bearing walls. Murphy kept the multi-gabled form of the original master ceiling and added white maple plywood paneling. Corrugated fiberglass doors on the wardrobe become a screen for backlit silhouettes of clothes at night, and the frosted-glass enclosure around the bathroom vanity displays other amorphous shapes.

The owners are avid cooks, so Murphy gave them a restaurant-style kitchen with commercial-grade appliances and stainless steel counters. Sliding doors open one end of the kitchen to the entry court.

White is predominant throughout: white fiberglass, white tile, white stucco, white clapboard siding, white steel sash windows, white steel details. "The house is really all about light and shadow," Murphy says.

Frosted-glass enclosures flanking the master vanity are lit from within coming alive at night with soft outlines of hanging clothes. William Mount

The fiberglass-paneled garage glows at night like a gigantic lantern. Murphy claims police helicopters use it for navigation. William Mount

The vaulted roof projects beyond the living room to cover the edge of the kidney-shaped pool, one of the few remnants of the original house. William Mount

In its concise planning and monochromatic shadings, the house adheres to a clear, focused vision, but Murphy, who briefly attended U.C.L.A. before dropping out to learn architecture as a builder (he even built some of Frank Gehry's early homes), has no identifiable style, and hopes to keep it that way.

"I once did a house . . . after being on the cover of a major design magazine . . . and the editor wouldn't run it," he recalls. "She said it was inconsistent with my 'style'! The only integrating theme I can see is that when you walk into one of my houses, the corners of your mouth turn up."

P erplexing, dynamic, breathtaking to behold, the Crawford house in Montecito, south of Santa Barbara, has a degree of intimacy not common to houses this large.

Architect Thom Mayne of Morphosis in Los Angeles credits his clients—an artist and her businessman husband who set out to build their dream home—for both tempering and encouraging his esoteric, challenging ideas about the nature of architecture.

The Crawfords wanted practical, comfortable living spaces, but they also wanted something more. They were fascinated by the primal power of ancient

Layered spaces lead to the front door, beyond the break in the concrete wall that defines the edge of the house. East-facing rooftop light monitors bring natural light inside. Richard Barnes

An entry opening in the wall aligns with the triangular pool that spills to a lower level and points toward the Pacific Ocean through a break in the house. The terrace is covered with multicolored African slate. Richard Barnes

Heating ducts are incorporated into vertical members of the house's steel frame, which form a rhythmic colonnade along the house's circulation spine. Richard Barnes

The living room is open to the kitchen and dining room beyond, with the transition between spaces emphasized by a drop in floor level. The fireplace is made of steel and smooth-troweled plaster. Richard Barnes

ruins at Stonehenge and Machu Picchu, and they asked for a house with similarly strong ties to the land. Also, they shared Mayne's interest in architecture that goes beyond practical issues such as siting, daylighting, and floorplans to expore more philosophical notions.

Nestled into its site, the 7800-square-foot house presents a low profile to the main neighborhood street on the east. Seven rooftop light monitors peak up through the trees in an orderly row to salute visitors approaching by car.

Morphosis conceived the house as four discrete, meticulously detailed pieces that break its substantial volume down to human scale. Three of these pieces—the studio/garage, main living space, and master suite—form the main house, and the fourth is a separate guest house.

The house offers a series of intimate experiences, beginning with a mysteriously layered entry procession that focuses on the distant Pacific Ocean as a magnetic attraction that pulls visitors through the spaces. Inside the house, a circulation spine runs along the back of the main floor, stringing together the master suite and central main living space, with its vaulted ceiling of Douglas fir plywood and latter-day Constructivist fireplace.

Douglas fir plywood is used on the vaulted ceiling in the main central living space, and on the dining room side of the fireplace. A granite kitchen prep island (foreground) faces the dining room. Richard Barnes

Instead of making the common wide-open California-style connection between the pool terrace and the house, Morphosis wanted the process of moving from outside to inside to be more mysterious. Nine pairs of concrete pylons help support the house, and some find expression in the rooftop light monitors.
Richard Barnes

An ocean-view 650-square-foot guest house tucked behind the main house continues the same palette of materials. A glass block wall encloses the shower.
Richard Barnes

Beyond the slate entry landing, the guest house interior is an inviting space that features exposed wood beams and shelves with grain that align with the entry axis.
Richard Barnes

Repeated forms and materials produce pleasing rhythms, from the orderly row of rooftop light monitors, whose redwood strips reappear on other parts of the house, to a series of exposed structural steel and redwood beams that skewer the house and guest house, to well-proportioned groups of squares and rectangles composed with the organic logic of traditional Japanese design. Earthy materials reinforce this natural aesthetic: steel, copper, concrete, clear redwood and Douglas fir plywood, exterior stucco in two shades of gray to emphasize wall planes, oak and slate flooring.

For Mayne, the Crawford house offered a chance to apply, on a much larger scale than earlier houses, a design process that ranged from practical concerns to poetic considerations, such as the three ordering systems that configure the house on its site.

The Mercator is an idealized map that organizes the world's land masses on a rectlinear grid. Mayne intended to lay out the Crawford house on such a perfect grid, but as he configured the buildings to the site and established floorplans, the structure didn't conform to this scheme, violating Mayne's attempt at order in a way that satisfied him.

Perpendicular primary lines of the house grew out of the site, with the main building stretching north-south to give every room an ocean view, and the main entry and pool strung along an east-west axis that points oceanward.

The guest bath has a custom concrete sink, tall glass doors that open to the shower, and a shower head mounted on the back of a central steel column. Richard Barnes

The Crawford house is set into the low, rolling hills of Montecito, where coastal fog drifts in on many days. The garage and owner's studio are in the far left portion of the house, the main living space is in the center, master suite at right, and the guest house in the foreground, beyond the steep-roofed period revival neighbor. Richard Barnes

Mayne circumscribed the 2.4-acre site with a circle, implied by sections of concrete wall around the house and guest house, with the house pushed to the eastern, uphill edge of the circle. "The placement of the building mass and wall is intended to complicate or reverse the relationship between center and periphery (a deserted center with life on the periphery?)," Mayne writes, illustrating how a building can raise philosophical and social issues.

"There's this very broad set of influences that has to do with the nature of our world today, the nature of communications, a pluralism that takes place beginning with one's education," adds Mayne, who earned architecture degrees from USC and Harvard. "Clearly the site-climate aspects of a regional territory bring a project specific information that influences the design, but that's not all that feeds the generative process. The work is about both global influences and the more traditional idea of considering specific circumstances."

Artist Sandy Bleifer likes the energy of Venice, the Los Angeles beach community that is home to artists, film people, assorted oddballs, and some of the city's most interesting architecture.

Bleifer and her husband, Ken, a physician, hired Los Angeles architect Frederick Fisher to design a house and studio for a 30-by-120-foot lot close to the Venice boardwalk. Bleifer's handmade paper collages sometimes depict gritty urban details. Fisher favors basic materials such as wood, brick, and concrete block. She sensed a shared aesthetic.

"I guess what my work has in common with Fred's is the use of natural materials for their own sake, for the look and the textures," she says. "Fred uses concrete block and doesn't cover it with stucco. I like his articulation of surfaces, the textures, the warmth of his spaces."

Fisher designed two separate buildings that share a center courtyard, with a glass-and-

A glass-and-steel bridge above a central courtyard connects the main house to Bleifer's studio. Windows ringing the court import natural light to both the house and studio. Marvin Rand

Within the narrow envelope of a lot near the Venice boardwalk, Fisher used low-key but ingeniously asymmetrical facades and a curved west wall that pulls away on both ends from a neighboring house to create a dynamic whole. Marvin Rand

From an open, second-level outlook, the double-height volume of the central living area is apparent. The long wall is a showplace for owner Sandy Bleifer's art. Marvin Rand

steel bridge connecting the structures. The front building contains a wide-open first floor living space and second-level master suite, while the back has guest quarters and home offices above Bleifer's studio. A basement wine cellar under the living room is reached by stairs that spiral down from the front courtyard.

Immediate and broader contexts both figured into Fisher's design.

"Lots in Venice are very narrow and symmetrical, but the larger setting is not symmetrical," Fisher says. "You have the mountains and city on one side, the ocean on the other. I tried to give the house a grain, if you will, so it doesn't feel equilateral, so it has inland and ocean sides."

The lot parallels the coastline, with the entry separated by a front courtyard from a public pedestrian walk. The east wall is covered with rough-textured stucco, in deference to the roughness of the city. West walls were troweled smooth as the surface of the Pacific on a calm day, including the bowed wall along the edge of the living room that moves away from a neighboring house to admit extra daylight.

Contrasts energize the interiors. Kitchen cabinets of maple and mahogany play off green and pinkish granite. Windows are placed to frame views and import light and are pleasing in their random variety. Refined materials in the house are countered by the utilitarian look of the studio, with its concrete floor and steel-frame windows.

The open central living space, which serves as kitchen, living room, and dining room, gets natural light from four directions. Kitchen counters are covered with granite. The stairs lead up to the master suite. Marvin Rand

In her studio, with its plentiful natural light and concrete floor, Bleifer makes paper from scratch and uses it to create large collages, some of them depicting decaying buildings. A guest room and Ken Bleifer's office are above the studio. Marvin Rand

Fisher believes the Bleifer house is the latest evidence of a maturing process that has continued since he left L.A. architect Frank Gehry's office in 1980.

"The Bleifer house is very complicated spatially and in terms of construction," he says. "But I think my compositional techniques and choices of materials are simpler. The earlier work was rougher in terms of construction, partly because those houses cost less. Over time I've tried to achieve the same ends with tighter technical resolution. I'm getting older and maybe my architecture is getting a bit more refined."

Airstream trailers and mobile homes dot the parched terrain at Joshua Tree, a tiny desert town twenty-five miles north of Palm Springs, where change comes only at glacial pace.

When Los Angeles architect Josh Schweitzer and five friends built this surreal weekend retreat, with its strong colors and unusual trapezoidal door and window openings, the place grabbed the attention of locals like a three-headed iguana.

But Schweitzer's house couldn't be more natural for the setting. He found his inspiration in the raw wind-burnished desert landscape. Sky blue, fiery sunset red, and the mossy green of low scrubby native plants define three primary cubic forms. Trapczoidal windows are abstractions of random spaces amid desert rock piles.

Morning light slants in to find visitors breakfasting in the northwest corner of the house at a wood table designed by Schweitzer, under a wavy hanging light he fashioned from inexpensive foam core. The double-height ceiling above living and dining areas allows daylight to filter down from windows ringing the second-story sleeping loft.

Afternoons, the mercury rises and visitors sprawl on beach chairs under the red pavilion, dousing each other with water to keep cool. They stay outside as twilight comes on cobalt blue, the temperature drops, and coals glow in a barbecue. During the hot months, Schweitzer sleeps in the pavilion.

Rooms are joined by plain openings, without doors. Materials are basic: wood, drywall, stucco, concrete aggregate floors. The house includes simple but pleasing details, such as the concrete bathroom vanity, stepping stones that repeat

Color on three cubes of this weekend getaway is drawn from desert sky, sunsets, and plant materials. The orangy open-air pavilion is an outdoor living room.
Tom Bonner

Trapezoidal openings frame desert views from within the pavilion. Schweitzer modeled the openings after random spaces he saw in desert rock formations. *Tom Bonner*

An open plan links the double-height living room with the dining room and kitchen beyond. Materials are basic, including an aggregate floor. Wayne Fujii

Schweitzer made the dining room light from foam core. Tom Bonner

The bedroom is a minimalist hideaway, with windows framing views like trapezoidal picture postcards. Tom Bonner

trapezoidal window shapes, and interior walls that join floors without cove base moldings.

Educated in architecture at the University of Kansas, Schweitzer worked briefly for Frank Gehry in Los Angeles before opening his own office, Schweitzer BIM, in 1984. His goal is to "derive new forms by creating volumes composed of flat planes and simple cutouts that avoid referencing past styles, industrial sentimentality, or engaging in anthropomorphism."

In the desert, Schweitzer has achieved a design free of clichés that suits the open expanses and simple rhythms of the environment. No phones or clocks can be found in this house, where mesmerizing patterns of light and shadow mark the movement of time.

Santa Monica Canyon is one of those rare patches of nature that still exist in odd corners of Los Angeles. Tucked among the canyon's mature old sycamores are innovative homes by architects including Richard Neutra, Raymond Kappe, and Brian Murphy.

L.A. architect Melinda Gray made her first mark here in the mid-eighties with a "calling card" house she designed for herself, and went on to design others nearby. The latest is this place for young attorneys Rod and Carolyn Guerra, which sums up the state of Gray's approach to architecture, a mix of solid craftsmanship, rational planning, and uninhibited experimentation.

"We wanted something open and airy, light and warm, also something that would have good flow for entertaining," Rod Guerra recalls. "We wanted to build this house for ourselves, with the ability to adapt to a family later as we had one. We told her we wanted a Southwestern home, but

The glass entry cube is tucked under an ocean-view deck. Cedar clapboards tie the house to nearby wooded areas in Santa Monica Canyon. Randall J. Corcoran

The kitchen looks out on the central courtyard (through door at left), and receives extra natural light through an opening to the hallway above. Randall J. Corcoran

The cylindrical courtyard carved out on the west side of this narrow lot brings natural light inside and is a great place to catch afternoon sun. Doors on the right lead to a family room. Randall J. Corcoran

Bowed lam beams support the vaulted roof, allowing an open second-floor interior. Randall J. Corcoran

French limestone covers walls and floors of the second-level master bath, which steals natural light from the hallway through a clerestory (just out of the photo to the left), and from windows lining the gable overhead. Randall J. Corcoran

Melinda came back with an alternative plan she thought might be better suited to the property. We thought it was beautiful."

Gray was schooled in architecture at U.C.L.A. and apprenticed with L.A. architect Anthony Lumsden, a disciplined designer of commercial structures. Her wilder side was nurtured during a brief mid-eighties stint in the office of L.A. architect Eric Moss, and her own designs often incorporate primary geometric shapes that collide and intersect in dynamic ways, organized by strong, logical plans.

"I'm really into order," Gray confesses as she sketches the plan for the Guerra house on a scrap of paper. "It affects people even if they don't perceive it. The whole idea of architecture is a subliminal order that

uplifts you in ways you may not always be aware of."

The basic layout of the Guerra residence is simple: two long, narrow volumes are joined along a central circulation spine, with three gabled "bootstraps" tying the volumes together on top. Six laminated wood beams, partially exposed inside, support a vaulted roof and minimize the need for load-bearing walls, allowing an open interior. A separate garage/guest quarters at the back of the lot echoes the home's three-story rear volume, and these two tall elements play off each other like sentries guarding the auto court.

Grid patterns help unify Gray's design. Squares of lawn grow up through precast concrete "Turf block" pavers. Checkerboards on exterior walls are defined by Douglas fir battens, and square wood windows and glass block capitalize on the theme.

While designing the new house for the Guerras, Payne lived on the site in its predecessor, a tiny cottage. She observed daily patterns of light and shade, climbed on the roof to get a firsthand look at potential views, and let her research shape the new house.

Most interior rooms get natural light from several directions. The third-floor study offers a peek at the Pacific, and a deck off the master bedroom perches atop the open entry tower, grabbing another glimpse of ocean.

First-floor family spaces include a dining room and kitchen at the east, where they catch morning light, and a living room and family room at the west, flanking a circular courtyard that pulls down extra daylight in this tight location.

Second-floor kids' rooms and a master suite are arranged along a hallway beneath the

vaulted roof. Rooms borrow space from other rooms. The back wall of the master shower, for instance, is high enough for privacy, but opens on top to the hall. The master bedroom has a big window that grabs light and space from the double-height living room but shuts out noise.

Contrasts animate the design: curved and straight lines, solids and voids, compact cozy volumes and soaring spaces. An open-riser wood-and-steel staircase sweeps up from the living room following the curve of the central courtyard, and other stairs spiral up through a cylindrical glass block

Gray used repeated square patterns to unify her design: turf block pavers set in the grass, battens applied to exterior in a grid pattern, and groups of square windows in a variety of sizes. Randall J. Corcoran

tower behind the courtyard. Cool stucco, steel, and limestone are set off by warm wood details and a second-floor carpet of natural fiber sisal.

Gray likes to experiment with materials. She gave the Guerra residence a base of smooth-troweled stucco, "the California substitute for stone," as she calls it, and she covered some exterior walls with marine plywood, painted pale gray to match the base. Natural-finish battens and sections of cedar clapboards help relate the house to its wooded canyon surroundings.

The end result is a formally mannered place that also has plenty of spunk. When Gray looks at the natty, well-organized exterior, she sees "a man dressed in solid pants, a striped shirt, and a checkered vest." No tie. After all, this is California.

Vernacular Australian homestead houses that open to big verandas, Virginia "flounder" houses that hug one side of a lot leaving the other for gardens, and Los Angeles traditions of indoor/outdoor living. These were some influences that went into the Santa Monica house architects Hank Koning and Julie Eizenberg designed for themselves and two children.

Their two-story house is formal outside, casual inside, conceived as four distinct elements intimately related to the landscape. The long 17-foot-wide main living wing is sited, flounder-style, along the north edge of the lot, leaving the south open for a sun-worshipping garden. An open wood-lathe garage and brick workshop anchor the back of the lot, which fronts a narrow alley.

Set back from the street behind greenery, covered with creeping vines, the front pavilion on the west end of the lot is skewed slightly off the property's lines to accommodate an inviting entry path along the north edge of the property, and to give first-floor living room windows more intimate views of the garden. The pavilion is covered with green stucco, softened by a vine-covered diagonal wire grid on the walls, another means of merging house and landscape.

Sliding glass doors open the corner of the living room to the garden. The treehouse-like second-level studio in the top of the front pavilion is ringed by narrow vertical wood windows, set between exposed 2-by-4 studs, and the architects can

A green entry pavilion with a criss-cross copper wire trellis is gradually receding into the landscape. Corner sliding doors open the first-floor living room to the garden. Tim Street-Porter

A wall of glass gives the south side of the house strong visual and circulation ties to the landscape, and an aluminum trellis will eventually be covered by a mix of creeping vines. Wayne Fujii

Glass-and-lattice entry connects the living room to the dining room beyond a broad opening that can be closed off with big sliding doors. Wayne Fujii

The kitchen/family room opens wide to the garden through a huge sliding window wall. Wayne Fujii

escape from work to a narrow widow's walk. Squares of light maple plywood and dark masonite make the checkerboard studio floor.

The kitchen/family room at the back of the house is the multipurpose core of the main living wing. A pantry joins the kitchen to the dining room, toward the front of the house. Stairs ascend from the family room to second-level bedrooms. Strip skylights bring daylight to an upstairs hall and the light spills down through the open stairwell to the first floor.

Koning and Eizenberg favor basic geometric forms bound by carefully balanced plans, tensioned by bold juxtapositions. The pavilion's deepeaved, nearly flat composition shingle roof is a springboard for the barrel-vaulted standing-seam metal roof over the main wing. An orderly row of four second-story windows along the south wall of the main wing, with concrete sills that defy weathering, serves as static counterpoint to the sliding-section window wall that merges the kitchen/family area with the garden.

The architects designed art and furniture, including wood inserts that expand the dining table, stored in plain view as essential pieces of a serving sideboard or mounted as geometric art above the fireplace. The fireplace was cast from smooth concrete imprinted with the forms and textures of eucalyptus leaves.

Koning and Eizenberg believe that in southern

Natural light spills down from the second floor through the stairwell to the first-floor family room. Wayne Fujii

The architects' second-level master bedroom has a pocket balcony and connects to their home studio. The vaulted ceiling is lined with stained sheet plywood. Wayne Fujii

The checkerboard studio floor is panels of light maple plywood and dark masonite. Green exposed framing and walls of glass help this elevated aerie merge with the treetops. The studio is surrounded by a widow's walk, beyond the yellow doors. Wayne Fujii

California, the landscape is as important as the structure. Wisteria, bougainvillea, trumpet, and grape vines climb a steel trellis that runs along the open garden side of the house. Assorted trees including eucalyptus at the edge of the garden provide privacy and a sense of enclosure, and various trees push up close to the studio aerie.

The architects came to Los Angeles in 1979 from Australia to attend graduate school in architecture at U.C.L.A., when Charles Moore was still on the faculty. They have since gained deep respect for early southern California Modern architects Irving Gill and R. M. Schindler, referring to them as "formal California Moderns," but they also admire Frank Gehry's more recent freeform designs.

They have assimilated some of the essential Modern architecture in Los Angeles, but they moved to the city with little knowledge of its architectural heroes, and they claim they have no manifestos or rigid expectations for the future, other than to pare their designs to basics.

"Coming here, we had no ambitions other than to land ourselves someplace else," claims Koning, who seems to be acclimating well to southern California.

SAN DIEGO

SD

RETROSPECTIVE

Gill's Klauber house (1907), a collaboration with Mead, mixed Gill's classic smooth walls and deep-set window openings with eclectic detailing such as lilting Oriental eaves. San Diego Historical Society, Photograph Collection

In 1907, Irving Gill electrified San Diego
with an architecture of bare essentials. Into
a city of a mere 40,000 that was a backward
burg compared with Los Angeles and San
Francisco, Gill dropped his first hard-edged assemblages of white cubic volumes, inspired by
California Mission imagery and his commitment
to developing new architecture suited to southern
California.

The Allen and Klauber houses marked the
emergence of a signature style that would become
his trademark during a brief prime that lasted for
only a decade. There must have been something
in the air in California in 1907 that caused the
state's architecture to make synchronous leaps.
Gill's architecture blossomed at the same time that
the brothers Greene were finishing the design of
the Gamble house (1908) in Pasadena, the ultimate Craftman manse. And in Berkeley in 1907,
Bernard Maybeck was completing drawings for the
Lawson house (1908), a finely detailed, understat-
ed Modern concrete structure that remains one of
his finest houses.

As was true of the Greenes and Maybeck, Gill
was also influenced by the Arts and Crafts movement that began during the late nineteenth century in England with architects including Voysey,
Lutyens, and Lethaby. Many of Gill's houses had
hardwood floors, thoughtful wood detailing, and
decorative tile, a simple natural richness that ran
counter to brocaded Victorianism. His houses also
had modern conveniences in keeping with the
Arts and Crafts quest for healthier living. Kitchen
disposals dropped garbage to basement incinera-
tors and vacuum cleaner wall outlets promoted
cleanliness.

In retrospect, among his California peers, Gill
is the one whose buildings now seem most
Modern in appearance, with their stark white
cubes stacked together like abstract sculptures.
Gill's first austere houses predated by nearly twenty
years the classic European Modern houses
designed by architects including Le Corbusier.
Gill's emergence paralleled that of Viennese archi-

*The Allen house (1907) in Bonita, codesigned by Gill and
Mead, marries Gill's Mission influences with Mead's love of
Mediterranean design. San Diego Historical Society, Photograph
Collection*

tect Adolf Loos, whose Steiner house (1910) is
cited by many historians as the earliest anti-orna-
ment house, a rebellion against elaborate neoclassical styles that had dominated the late nineteenth
century.

Like Maybeck in Berkeley and the Greenes in
Los Angeles, Gill had strong feelings for the qualities of his region (his Los Angeles houses are covered in the L.A. section of this book). He also had
a broader social and philosophical agenda that
included innovative ideas about marrying buildings to landscapes, creating well-designed, low-cost
social housing, and experimenting with materials.
His fresh intellectual perspectives, expressed in
articles he wrote for *The Craftsman* magazine, realized in numerous buildings, made Gill genuinely
Modern, not just a designer who hit on a pleasing
marriage of Mission and Arts and Crafts styles.

Gill's finest San Diego houses exist now only
as visions provoked by faded photos, wrin-
kled plans, and old articles from *The
Craftsman*. The best of his San Diego houses,
designed between 1907 and 1915, were demol-
ished during the 1960s and 1970s, including the

The minimalist Timken house (1907) was at the cutting edge at a time when rustic Craftsman was the hot California style. San Diego Historical Society, Photograph Collection

Timken and Klauber houses. Black-and-white documents can't give the full three-dimensional picture, but there's no mistaking the revolutionary nature of Gill's architecture.

His writings reveal his commitment to inventing a new architecture suited to southern California.

"If we, the architects of the West, wish to do great and lasting work we must dare to be simple, must have the courage to fling aside every device that detracts the eye from the structural beauty, must break through convention and get down to fundamental truths," he wrote in *The Craftsman*.

In 1911, Craftsman, Victorian, and imported East Coast styles dominated residential design in San Diego. So the house Gill created for roller-bearing entrepreneur Henry Timken was certifiably radical. Situated a few blocks west of Balboa Park, this flat-roofed home consisted of simple cubic volumes punctuated by square and rectangular window openings. The house was arranged in a *U* around a courtyard, with living and dining rooms flanking the court. Inviting sequences of indoor and outdoor spaces guided visitors from the house into the landscape.

Gill's plans for the house make it obvious that he thought indoor and outdoor spaces should be integrally planned, with intimate visual and circulation connections. A series of everexpanding spaces made a methodical, pleasing transition from indoors to out, tied together by a central circulation axis that swept through the house and courtyard into a large, geometrically arranged back garden included on Gill's drawings.

From the sidewalk in front of the Timken house, visitors followed a walkway to a covered porch, a compact, cozy portal. Beyond the front door, a wide entrance hall welcomed them into its more expansive space, and French doors led to a covered loggia, where columns framed a view of a fountain at the center of the courtyard. The courtyard was built as a roofless outdoor room, complete with walls. Windows in the back wall framed views of the garden beyond.

"It would be difficult to imagine a more interesting example of a house built around a court than one recently completed in San Diego for Henry H. Timkin [sic]," wrote Eloise Roorbach in a 1913 issue of *The Craftsman*. "This house sets a new standard for home-building. It embodies the most advanced ideas of design and construction. The desire of some home-makers for perfect simplicity of design, combined with a substantial form

The Timken house (1907) was one of Gill's earliest stripped-to-basics designs and featured strong indoor-outdoor ties. San Diego Historical Society, Photograph Collection

of construction, has in this house been fully realized. Not a single ornament mars the pure symmetry of its lines."

Gill's objective was to omit nonessentials, and the result was a pure, unornamented sculptural house. But even in its austerity, the house captured some Mission-era romance, striking a delicate balance between California's Hispanic past and the Modern future of architecture. The courtyard was paved with 12-inch terra-cotta tiles, and the fountain gurgled in the quiet, protected space, protected from insects by an overhead copper screen. Vines twisted around columns, ferns reposed in shady beds, and flowering plants exhaled sweet fragrance.

Details were indicative of Gill's obsession with sanitation. Woodwork was flush with walls, elimating ledges where dust could accumulate, and kitchen counters and bathtub surrounds were of magnesite, a stone-like material molded in a curve to make a one-piece transition from flat surface to wall, leaving no seams where bacteria, insects, and dirt could hide.

Gill's plans were nowhere near as open or imaginative as Wright's from the same period, nor his use of space as progressive as Schindler's in Los Angeles a few years later, but Gill was ahead of his time in his spare, minimal approach and use of cross ventilation, enhanced daylighting through skylights and generous glazing, and experimental materials including concrete.

Known as a charismatic ladies' man who liked to go dancing at the Hotel Del Coronado, Gill had great success considering the progressive nature of his designs. He designed several houses each year during his prime decade, amazing considering the size and cultural conservatism of the city. But San Diego's infatuation with Gill was short-lived. Beginning with the 1915 Panama-California Exposition in Balboa Park, which featured Spanish Colonial revival buildings designed by Bertram Goodhue and others, San Diegans increasingly favored the romance of traditional Mediterranean styles, which dominated for the next thirty years as Gill's commissions dwindled. At the time of his death in 1936, he was picking avocados to earn extra money, and his occupation was listed on his death certificate as "laborer."

Young San Diego architects still find inspiration in Gill's architecture, not so much in the forms but in his sense that southern California had qualities—the climate, the light, the lifestyle, the culture, the terrain—that could be addressed by new types of houses.

Geographically, San Diego County is similar to Los Angeles, ranging from flat oceanfront areas such as Mission Beach and Pacific Beach to hillier coastal towns like La Jolla and Del Mar and rugged, low inland hills, valleys, and canyons. Original vegetation was sparse, but imported water has made some parts of the city virtually as green as areas in northern California.

San Diego architects whose recent designs are included in this book look to the terrain and climate for important cues, and some still feel connected to the area's early Hispanic heritage of missions and low ranch houses around courtyards. But one predominant trend is an increasing focus on the micro-region. Many of these architects find inspiration in the immediate contexts of neighborhoods. They want their houses to be more than shelters and not easily classifiable, and they are exploring new ways of charging them with layers of meaning.

As in Los Angeles, the newest wave of innovative San Diego architecture began emerging during the late seventies, when architects such as Rob Wellington Quigley, Ted Smith, Randy Dalrymple, and Tom Grondona began exploring new ways to respond to their region, drawing from assorted local sources, conscious of both immediate settings and larger geographical contexts, with a shared interest in bringing humor, free forms, and a broader philosophical agenda to their designs.

Smith, for example, collages assorted forms and materials from neighborhood buildings into his houses, with an effect that can seem both familiar and new. Grondona takes an artist's approach to design, creating houses through a spontaneous process of drawing, model-making, sometimes inventing imaginative fables to explain how his houses were created.

Quigley's approach parallels Frank Gehry's in Los Angeles, and developed during the same period. Gehry's radical remodel of his Santa Monica house, incorporating such unlikely materials as chain-link fencing and wired glass, was completed in 1978. Quigley's Squire residence in Del Mar was completed the following year and elevates common materials such as asphalt shingle and concrete block to rich residential purpose. Like Grondona, Quigley made use of mythic pasts he invented for sites to spur his imagination. He imagined that the Squire residence, for example, was built around the ruins of a 1000-year-old wall, and this fable imbued the house with some castle-like qualities, including a concrete block fireplace and wall with an arched opening.

As these architects continue to evolve, another generation is emerging, conscious of San Diego's architectural heritage, but not bound by it, also aware that the work of architects such as Quigley, Grondona, Dalrymple, and Smith in San Diego and others nationally and internationally paved the way during the eighties for freer expression in the nineties.

While many of the San Diego architects included in this book are still in their thirties, young for a profession where maturity often doesn't manifest until much later, they are already displaying a great deal of sophistication in the way forms and materials come together, whether their houses are freely sculptural and expressionistic, like Jeanne McCallum's place for two artists, or quieter, like the La Jolla house designed by Wallace Cunningham. Even the wildest houses in this book come across as solid evidence that their architects are knowledgeable about materials and the structurally sound, aesthetically pleasing ways they can be put together. One thing lacking in some of this new work from younger architects is the kind of complexity Quigley et al achieved early on. Though their buildings were often carelessly crafted, the ideas behind them were rich.

Brad Burke and Eric Naslund, partners in a company called Studio E, whose own houses are included in this book, support the idea of regional architecture and have closely examined Gill's designs, elements of which seem relevant to their own work.

"I don't think regionalism is a style thing," Burke says. "For me there are three basic compo-

nents: physical (sensitivity to land form), climatic (controlling natural elements to promote indoor/outdoor living), and cultural (recognizing the architectural traditions and lifestyle synonymous with southern California). There's a definite regional interest beginning to show itself in San Diego."

Burke admires the way Gill adapted the architecture of the California missions: "Clean wall planes, usually out of stucco, that let you do a lot of things with light and shadow, simple massing, the way light enters a house, where window openings are placed, cross ventilation, outdoor spaces that serve as usable extensions of rooms."

Burke's house looks nothing like houses designed by Gill, yet it accomplishes some similar tasks. The house makes optimal use of its site, and it deals efficiently with daylighting, fresh air, and relating indoors to usable outdoor space (in Burke's case, a compact deck).

Tall and composed of volumes arranged slightly off kilter from a standard rectilinear grid, Naslund's house, too, looks nothing like a Gill. Yet the way it wraps around an old mock orange tree in a courtyard echoes courtyard homes designed by Gill, including the Timken house in San Diego and the Dodge house in Los Angeles. Naslund has learned from Gill the raw power of plain stucco walls punctuated only by windows, arranged for daylighting purposes, not appearance.

Smith also finds Gill to be a heroic figure, although Smith's architecture bears no resemblance to Gill's. Smith believes in regionalism, but he finds his inspiration more in neighborhoods than in broader social or geographical contexts or famous Modern architects of the past.

"The thing that's so good about Gill, he took the Modern white box and put the Spanish arch on it," Smith says. "It's the perfect example of being in the world culture and in the region at the same time.

"I like the idea of regionalism because I like the idea of building a place, building on what you've got, richening what you already have to make it better instead of divergent," says Smith, who uses the word *blendo* to describe his contextual collaging. "What I'm doing with the blendo thing is trying to go with the house next door, to get some visual affinity, and that's as much regionalism as I can come up with. At the same time, it's nice to have a deeper dream of a place like San Diego, like Gill was doing."

Compared with Los Angeles and San Francisco, San Diego was small and isolated through the first half of the century, and retains some of this provincialism. In 1992 the city gained its first major university architectural program (at U.C. San Diego), but it closed the following year, a casualty of the state budget crunch. The city has never been home to cosmopolitan, artistic types, especially from the movie world, who became the clients of Modern architects in Los Angeles. Early twentieth-century Modern architects such as Schindler, Neutra, and their protégés in Los Angeles had strong European ties, giving their architecture a broader range of sources. The evolving Modern architecture was reinforced by strong architectural institutions, including the architecture school at U.S.C. Maybeck, Wurster, Esherick, and others in the Bay Area, partially through their connection with the University of California, were also conversant with the latest Modern design ideas from the East Coast and Europe.

"San Diego has always been a cultural cul de sac," Quigley says, theorizing that the city's shortage of direct contact with international arts and culture might have worked partially to the city's advantage, allowing San Diego architects room to develop creative, individual responses to their place.

It is exactly this relative provincialism that has attracted promising architects to San Diego from elsewhere, such as Christine Killory and Rene Davids, who moved to San Diego in 1987 from England, and whose own house is included in this book.

"It seemed more isolated than Los Angeles and there seemed to be greater opportunities," says Davids. "There were less groups or cliques or vested interests."

Just as the architects in this book search for ways to incorporate a variety of influences into designs especially suited to San Diego,

so Gill was a product of diverse influences. Born in either 1870 or 1873 in Syracuse, New York, he became an architect without a formal education in architecture, launching his career in the Chicago office of Adler and Sullivan at a time when architects there were using new steel technology to revolutionize the design of tall buildings.

Gill worked in Chicago for two years during the early 1890s. He witnessed the dramatic, organic potential of arches while working in Sullivan's Chicago office, at which time he undoubtedly also saw rusticated stone buildings on the East Coast designed by Sullivan's mentor, Henry Hobson Richardson, many of which prominently featured arches. According to Esther McCoy, in her book *Five California Architects*, Sullivan "turned the faces of the young men away from Europe and bade them look to Africa, a land of the serene wall, of earth forms, of decorative details." African sources would crop up again for Gill many years later, beginning during his brief partnership in San Diego with Frank Mead.

When Gill arrived in San Diego in 1893, the city was in a recession and the population was only 17,000. Gill designed his first San Diego house in 1893, a mix of neoclassical and Victorian elements that gave no hint of his Modern potential. He became partners in 1898 with architect William Hebbard, who had worked for Birnham and Root in Chicago during the 1890s.

By the time he designed a small house for himself in 1904, Gill was already paring his architecture to essentials and experimenting with new methods of construction. He built some interior walls using 1-by-4 studs 4 inches apart covered with diagonal lathing and plaster, which produced walls 3 inches thick that were equal in strength to conventional 2-by-4 frame walls 5 1/2 inches thick. His houses often had floors of bare concrete, tinted with mixes of yellow, red, or brown pigment, waxed to a satin sheen.

When Gill opened his own office in 1906, his signature architecture began emerging. San Diego architect Mead made a significant, oft-overlooked contribution to the evolution of Gill's stripped down, mature style. Mead visited North Africa in 1903 and came back inspired by Islamic architecture including white flat-roofed, smooth-walled houses with simple punched door and window openings. He became Gill's partner in 1907, and their collaboration yielded three houses.

The Klauber house of 1907 (torn down in 1979) had smooth white walls of concrete and hollow tile, arched openings, and flourishes such as a gabled roof with an oriental flare to the eaves. Walls were covered with creeping vines, and vine-covered trellises linked the house to the landscape.

Also in 1907, Mead and Gill designed the Bailey house in La Jolla, with barn doors that slid open to a vine-covered pergola, a radical merger of indoors and outdoors achieved fifteen years before R. M. Schindler's open home/studio in Hollywood.

The 1907 Allen house in Bonita, another Gill/Mead design, was an important step in Gill's evolution, a concrete box punctuated by evenly spaced windows and pierced by openings in the front facade for the entry porch and a second-level balcony.

Gill's emerging philosophy was that truth in architecture could be found in extreme economy and understatement. To him, this meant not only leaving off ornament, but using a few rhythmically repeated forms he found in nature, as he explained in *The Craftsman*:

"The straight line borrowed from the horizon is a symbol of greatness, grandeur and nobility; the arch patterned from the dome of the sky represents exultation, reverence, aspiration; the circle is the sign of completeness, motion and progression, as may be seen when a stone touches water; the square is the symbol of power, justice, honesty and firmness. These are the bases, the units of architectural language, and without them there can be no direct or inspired architectural speech."

Arches became a Gill trademark, adding curves that softened the hard-edged rectangular and square forms he preferred during his prime. He often used arched arcades as transitional spaces between interiors and landscapes.

He built his pure, simple forms from stucco, hollow tile filled with concrete, or solid concrete. He developed tilt-slab concrete techniques, pouring walls in forms on the ground with steel door and window frames in place, tilting the cured walls into place with a system of pulleys and cables that allowed a few workers to hoist a heavy wall. Gill used tilt-slab construction both for houses and for other buildings including the 1913 La Jolla Women's Club, his best-known remaining structure in San Diego.

Gill was fascinated with the idea of new, efficient interiors.

"In California we have long been experimenting with the idea of producing a perfectly sanitary, labor-saving house, one where the maximum of comfort may be had with the minimum of drudgery," he wrote in the May 1916 issue of *The Craftsman*. "In the recent houses that I have built, the walls are finished flush with the casings and the line where the wall joins the flooring is slightly rounded, so that it forms one continuous piece with no place for dust to enter or to lodge, or crack for vermin of any kind to exist. There is no molding for pictures, plates or chairs, no baseboard, paneling or wainscoting to catch and hold the dust. The doors are single slabs of hand-polished mahogany swung on invisible hinges or else made so that they slide into the wall. In some of the houses all windows and door frames are of steel."

Gill was increasingly aware of the potential for joining interiors to gardens through the use of courtyards, French doors, pergolas, and arched arcades. He never intended his most austere houses to remain that way. His idea was that pristine wall surfaces uninterrupted by decoration or other finicky detail could provide the perfect backdrop for lush California gardens. In the oft-quoted *Craftsman* article he wrote in 1916, he said:

"We should build our house simple, plain and substantial as a boulder, then leave the ornamentation of it to Nature, who will tone it with lichens, chisel it with storms, make it gracious and friendly with vines and flower shadows as she does the stone in the meadow."

In 1916, the last of Gill's minimalist white houses in San Diego was completed, the Scripps residence in La Jolla, the remains of which are now embedded within the San Diego Museum of Contemporary Art's building in La Jolla. Ironically, plans to expand the museum with an addition designed by Philadelphia architect Robert Venturi call for the original facade of the Scripps residence to be recreated as part of the renovated structure.

The last minimal Modern house designed by Gill in San Diego: the Scripps residence in La Jolla (1916). San Diego Historical Society, Photograph Collection

For decades after Gill's death in 1936, well into the seventies, the significance of the flat-roofed, cubistic houses he designed in San Diego and Los Angeles during his prime was underrecognized.

In Los Angeles, Gill was an important link in a chain of architects exploring new ways of addressing an emerging new culture in relatively flat, open, sparsely populated territory. Chronologically and stylistically, Gill served as a vital bridge between the brothers Greene and R. M. Schindler (he knew Schindler and passed on tips about concrete) and several younger Modern architects who came later. But in San Diego, Gill stands out as a lone, heroic figure of Modern architecture between the turn of the century and the years after World War II.

Gill was mentioned by critics in major tomes on Modern architecture, but, along with Maybeck in Berkeley and Schindler in Los Angeles, was seldom seen on an equal footing with top European Modernists including Loos and Le Corbusier. Aside from Esther McCoy, in her 1960 book *Five California Architects*, few writers gave Gill more than a paragraph or two.

Lewis Mumford, the granddad of American architecture critics, was aware of Gill's significance. In the introduction to his 1952 book *Roots of Contemporary Architecture*, Mumford hailed Gill as "a bold pioneer on the West Coast—well in advance of the purism of Le Corbusier and Ozenfant."

In his 1958 book *Architecture: Nineteenth and Twentieth Centuries*, the famous New York architectural historian Henry-Russell Hitchcock devoted far less space to Gill than to Modern European architects, including Adolf Loos, Gill's contemporary, although Hitchcock did note that Gill's houses "have a deceptive air of being European rather than American and of a period some years later than that in which they were actually built." This was his roundabout way of admitting that Gill was ahead of his time.

"In his best work . . . the asymmetrically organized blocks, crisply cut by windows of various sizes carefully sashed and disposed, with roof terraces or flat roofs above, more than rival the contemporary houses of the Austrian architect Adolf Loos in the abstract distinction of the composition. They even approach rather closely the most advanced European houses of the next decade," Hitchcock wrote.

"Gill's interiors are especially fine and also quite like Loos's. Very different from the rich orientalizing rooms designed by the Greenes, they are in fact more similar to real Japanese interiors in their severe elegance. The walls of fine smooth cabinet woods, with no mouldings at all, are warm in colour, and Voysey-like wooden grilles of plain square spindles give human scale. The whole effect, in its clarity of form and simplicity of means, is certainly more premonitory of the next stage of modern architecture than any other American work of its period."

More recently, Gill has not been so well treated. Charles Jencks's standard architecture school text *Modern Movements in Architecture* (1973) makes no mention of him, and Kenneth Frampton's *Modern Architecture: A Critical History* (1980) only cites Gill's name in passing, without detailing his architecture.

In 1982, British critic William Curtis took a more enlightened view of Gill in his book *Modern Architecture Since 1900*, another "must" for architecture students.

". . . Gill's was no mere grass roots romanticism: his work was motivated by a social vision of considerable breadth," Curtis wrote. "He thought of California as the last frontier, and therefore a suitable place for the expression of a new way of life based on the best of old American democratic ideals. The significance of stripped simplicity in his work was therefore partly moral, but very far in its meanings from the machine idolization of the avant-garde in Europe who were to create the modern movement of the twenties."

Gill's fleeting popularity after 1916 and the predominance of assorted Mission and Mediterranean revival styles of architecture, along with imported East Coast styles in San Diego, illustrate the slow progress made by Modern architecture in the city, for reasons one can only speculate about. For the first forty-five years of this century, Gill was the only architect who produced a body of innovative Modern architecture. From the twenties until well into the forties, residential architects who are still considered San Diego's finest from that period worked primarily in assorted Mediterranean revival modes.

One reason for the lack of experimental architecture may be that San Diego's population grew more slowly than the populations of Los Angeles and the San Francisco Bay Area. San Diego had a population of 40,000 in 1908, whereas Los Angeles had passed 100,000 in 1900 and San Francisco was home to 342,782 by 1900. According to some historians, the people who came to southern California were a different mix than those who migrated to San Francisco. Many of the new southern Californians were from small rural towns in the Midwest, whereas those who moved to San Francisco tended to be more urbane types from big eastern cities such as Boston and New York.

"Architecturally, San Diego has exported three great commodities—the rationalist approach of Irving J. Gill, the Spanish Colonial Revival via the 1915 Exposition, and more recently the Jack-in-the-Box restaurant," wrote historian David Gebhard in his *A Guide to Architecture in Los Angeles and Southern California.*

After working for Gill, several architects went on to do strong architecture of their own in San Diego, though none were as prolific or creative as Gill.

Weaver moved from Chicago to San Diego in 1903, and houses such as the Strong residence (1907), combined Prairie and Craftsman influences. San Diego Historical Society, Photograph Collection

Emmor Brooke Weaver went to work for Gill in 1903, and eventually designed several fine Craftsman-style houses on his own that featured elaborate wood joinery along the lines of Greene and Greene in Los Angeles. Weaver never went to Gill's stripped-down extremes, but houses such as the Strong residence (1907) show how he combined Craftsman elements with smooth stucco walls, also how he recognized the relevance of integrating indoors and outdoors in California. The Strong house has a broad second-level veranda that offers a bird's-eye view of the street and serves as an extension of indoor space, and the O'Neall house on Spruce Street has a long, covered front porch that serves as transitional space between the garden and the interior entry hall. Some of Weaver's houses are dark at the core, but his plans have open, flowing Modern tendencies.

Hazel Waterman went into architecture after her husband died and left her with three children to support. She was thirty-seven, it was 1903, and, with encouragement from Gill, who had designed a stone cottage for Waterman and her husband, Waldo, she learned drafting by taking correspondence courses.

Waterman was no stranger to design, having studied art at U.C. Berkeley, also writing about architecture as early as 1902 for *The House Beautiful* magazine. She learned architecture as a draftswoman for Hebbard and Gill, and designed her first houses while still with Gill's office in 1906. Waterman's houses covered a variety of styles, from Craftsman houses and related English cottage structures with steep roofs, deep eaves, and half timbering, to her Italianate design of the

Ackerman residence (1912), with its columned entry and clay tile roof, and the Clayton residence (1909), which, with its green-shuttered windows, brick first floor, and clapboard second story looked like an East Coast import.

While she never had much chance to exercise it on a residential commission, Waterman shared Gill's fascination with advancing Mission architecture to a spare, Modern approach. She supervised the restoration of the Casa de Estudillo, a nineteenth-century adobe in San Diego, and she designed several nonresidential buildings, including the Wednesday Club on East Ivy Lane in San Diego that had crisp white stucco walls, simple orderly window placement, and outdoor pergolas reminiscent of Gill's

While Waterman's body of residential work wasn't nearly as prolific or progressive as Gill's, she used Mission elements to design buildings that were well suited to the climate and Hispanic cultural heritage of San Diego. Waterman's house plans often included garden designs, assuring that her buildings would be sensitively sited and intimately related to the surrounding landscape, ideas that were vital to California's early Modern architects, including Gill and Schindler.

Frank Mead and Richard Requa both worked for Gill, then formed a partnership in 1912.

Mead's travels through Africa and various Mediterranean areas and Requa's trips to Italy, Spain, and Africa gave the pair a deep knowledge of Mediterranean design, which they believed could be perfectly adapted to San Diego. Like Gill and Schindler, Mead was very familiar with the pueblo dwellings of the American Southwest, having spent three years working for an Apache tribe's territorial rights in Arizona.

During the twenties, Requa published two books of photos and writings chronicling his trips to the Mediterranean.

In one of these, published in 1929 by the Monolith Portland Cement Co. and titled *Old World Inspiration for American Architecture*, Requa stated that his goal was "to provide worthy examples of Old World architecture that will stimulate the development of appropriate styles in America."

Requa believed Mediterranean houses were sensitively tailored to their locales and functions, and he took a Modern view of the design process:

Hopi House (1914) was Mead and Requa's take on pueblos of the Southwest. In back is an earlier design by Mead and Gill. San Diego Historical Society, Photograph Collection

Function before form. He did not condone the idea of choosing a style then making essential uses, or rooms, fit.

"The result is a forced and more or less impracticable interior dressed in an inappropriate, academic exterior dictated by the rules and dimensions of the designer's ritual," he wrote. "Seldom is such a building in harmony with its environment or a true expression of its materials and purposes. Its alien ancestry is offensively obvious. Lack of inspiration and ingenuity results in banal, spiritless imitation without character or reason.

"A building cannot approach perfection from the standpoint of utility or art, if the plan and structural requirements are made subservient to its design and decorative treatment.

"There must be harmony between plan and design, between design and environment, between beauty and utility."

Requa found only two architectural approaches in use in the United States that met his requirements: the Indian pueblos of the Southwest, and the early adobes of California.

Mead and Requa designed a few stark, boxy houses similar to some of Gill's, but the Sweet house, completed in 1914, is the most extraordinary of their houses. Historians give Mead more credit for the architecture, which is tightly integrated with a landscape by Paul Thiene.

The house sits at the top of its sloping site on Bankers Hill, with sweeping views of downtown

Mead and Requa's masterpiece: The Sweet house (1914). San
Diego Historical Society, Photograph Collection

*The sun room at the Sweet house opened wide through several
glass doors to a terrace.* San Diego Historical Society, Photograph
Collection

and San Diego Bay, and is kept in its original con-
dition, including furnishings, by Kathleen
Stoughton, its current owner. The house is surrounded by a tall stucco wall, in the Mediterranean tradition of blank street-facing walls that
seclude dwellings from street noise and add
romantic mystery. Eclectic detailing includes a
deep keyhole-shaped Moorish doorway and modest arched entry in the garden wall. The range of
types of arches—round, pointed, horseshoe-
shaped—are evidence of influences ranging from
Gill and the missions to Mead and Requa's
Moorish travels.

Yet certain elements were in sync with the
emerging Modern architecture of the period,
especially Gill's: simple cubic massing; lack of decoration on wall surfaces; open interior planning;
and strong visual and circulation connections to
the landscape.

A covered sun porch with an open-beam ceiling, for example, looks out on a terrace through
several sets of redwood-framed glass doors lining
two walls. Opening the doors transforms the
room into an open-air pavilion, more aggressively
connected to the outdoors even than houses from
this period designed by Gill or the brothers
Greene in Los Angeles. The living room has large
sliding wood-and-glass pocket doors on one side
that open to the sun porch, and French doors
flanking the fireplace in the south wall admit garden views and plenty of daylight. One of these sets

of doors leads out to a vine-covered pergola along
the edge of a formal garden. Several Phillipine
mahogany French doors in the dining room also
open to the garden.

Requa, who died in 1941, continued to design
houses of assorted Mediterranean derivation
through the twenties, but his attentions were
increasingly devoted to nonresidential projects.

Lilian Rice was born in National City, south
of San Diego, and was one of the first
women to graduate from the University of
California's architecture school (in 1910). In San
Diego, she worked for partners Richard Requa and
Herbert Jackson, both former draftsman for Gill,
and her greatest contribution to San Diego County
was master planning downtown Rancho Santa Fe
and designing roughly sixty residences there, most
of them in Mediterranean Revival styles.

Like Gill and Waterman, Rice was enamored
of Mediterranean elements, especially the use of
courtyards as cool, quiet oases hidden from the
street by blank stucco walls. With her formal architectural education and experience in planning,
Rice was concerned with siting sympathetically
with the surrounding terrain, and relating her
houses to nature.

Rice's houses, with their stucco walls and tile
roofs, seem traditional, but if you imagine a design
such as the 1928 Hamilton Carpenter residence in

Rice designed several clean-lined Mediterranean houses in Rancho Santa Fe, including the Hamilton Carpenter residence (1928). San Diego Historical Society, Photograph Collection

Mission Hills houses of the 1930s designed by William Templeton Johnson and others showed the growing domination of Mediterranean styles. San Diego Historical Society, Photograph Collection

Rancho Santa Fe without its tile roof, it could just as well be a Gill house, with its crisp cubic volumes, pristine planes of white stucco, and deep-set arched and square window and door openings.

During the twenties, when architects such as Wurster, Dailey, and Esherick in the Bay Area and Schindler, Neutra, and others in Los Angeles worked in Modern directions, without historical references, searching for fresh responses to their regions, top architects including William Templeton Johnson practicing in San Diego continued with variations on Mediterranean Revival: courtyards, tile roofs, deep-set windows, white stucco walls, and ornate wrought iron and polychromatic tile decoration. Some of the plans hinted at Modern open planning, with rooms flowing freely together through wide openings, and some of the houses featured strong visual and circulation ties between indoor and outdoor spaces. In appearance, though, these were strictly traditional. There were a couple of isolated 1930s incidents of Streamline Moderne, a curvaceous variation on Art Deco, but after Gill, Modernism didn't really gain momentum again until after World War II. One reason is that the Depression and World War II put a damper on construction.

uring and after the war, however, construction of new housing exploded to meet the demand created by the influx of military families and workers employed by the booming aircraft industry, and Lloyd Ruocco was the unsung architectural hero of the early postwar years in San Diego.

Ruocco was educated in architecture at U.C. Berkeley during the 1920s (when the school was still under the the the classical influence of the French École des Beaux-Arts), where Maybeck, an early instructor at Berkeley, had been educated.

During the 1930s, Ruocco was a draftsman in Rice's office, and later also worked for Requa and for William Templeton Johnson. Ruocco's houses were regional in the sense that they responded to local terrain and weather and used materials available in San Diego, but he was more influenced by internationally known Modern architects than by Irving Gill.

"He looked up to Frank Lloyd Wright and Schindler, and he was very aware of the great European Modern architects, such as Mies and Corbu," says Tom Robertson, who lives in a San Diego house Ruocco designed around 1942 that was finally built after the war.

Robertson's house was one of Ruocco's earliest residential designs. It is earthy, low, and crafted from redwood columns, beams, and paneling, but it is also Modern in its openness, liberal use of glass, indoor/outdoor connections, and subtle indirect lighting.

The concrete-floored living room, for example, has two walls of glass, and one of these incor-

In the 1940s, Ruocco broke nearly thirty years of Mediterranean Revivals with his Modern houses. Douglas M. Simmonds

In 1976, when he designed his own house, Ruocco was still committed to modular post-and-beam construction. Douglas M. Simmonds

porates a huge wood-framed sliding door that opens to a patio. Redwood columns around the room hold up redwood beams big enough to support the roof without interior columns, leaving the big room uncluttered. Ruocco tucked indirect lighting fixtures above soffits at the edges of the room, and placed clerestory windows above the soffits to supply additional daylighting.

Ruocco was an admirer of the Case Study Houses program that flourished in Los Angeles during the 1950s and early 1960s under the leadership of John Entenza, editor of *Arts and Architecture* magazine. Ruocco was especially interested in the possibility of constructing houses from standard prefabricated parts, as were such Case Study architects as Pierre Koenig.

One of Ruocco's most inspiring designs was an experimental steel and glass house erected in Balboa Park in 1976 as part of San Diego's celebration of America's Bicentennial. Ruocco wanted the house to prove the viability of simple modular construction, and he designed it in prefabricated steel-framed sections that bolted together.

When the Bicentennial celebration was over, Ruocco moved the house to a lot near San Diego State University. He sited it, in Wrightian fashion, not at the top of his sloping lot, near the street, but lower on the hill, so the house was invisible from the street and more intimately connected to the natural setting.

The house had walls of huge glass panels and a central courtyard shaded by movable canvas awnings. At the center of the living room was a freestanding fireplace with a cylindrical stainless-steel chimney that extended through the ceiling and radiated heat through the room. Some walls rose only partway to the ceiling, with glass spanning the gap, so that rooms borrowed space and light from adjacent rooms.

Other Ruocco houses featured conveniences that are taken for granted now, but which were progressive during the 1950s and 1960s, such as private exercise rooms and built-in floor-to-ceiling cabinets with fold-out desks.

Ruocco preserved existing trees on various lots, letting them grow up through holes in decks or brush up against exterior walls. When materials were difficult to come by or clients had modest budgets, Ruocco improvised with whatever was available. His San Diego Design Center building on Fifth Avenue had retaining walls made of concrete fragments from old city streets, and he sometimes used plywood for ceilings and walls and masonite for floors.

Homer Delawie, Paul McKim, and Russell Forester were among top young San Diego architects of the 1950s who found great inspiration in Ruocco's designs.

"If there was anybody I could hang a hat on, it was Lloyd Ruocco," says Forester, who designed several Modern houses during the 1950s and went on to create the prototype Jack-in-the-Box restaurant.

Forester met Ruocco in 1942, when the two were draftsmen for a company building Navy ships in San Diego. Forester remembers Ruocco, who died in 1981, as a philosopher-architect with an imaginative approach to design. Ruocco's first house was along organic lines, with walls of tamped earth.

"But his other houses were steel and glass and very much what I'd call International Style," Forester says, referring to the movement that began in 1932 with the International Style show of Modern architects at the Museum of Modern Art in New York, organized by architect Phillip Johnson and critic Henry-Russell Hitchcock.

North of San Diego, John Lloyd Wright (who died in 1972), the great master's son, lived in the tiny coastal city of Del Mar and designed several houses there and elsewhere in southern California, carrying on the spirit of the master. Wright (who invented Lincoln Logs) apprenticed with his father, working on projects that included the Imperial Hotel in Tokyo. His own house, completed in 1947, was crafted of brick and wood, but he also designed crisp, clean-lined houses in stucco, such as the McPherson house of 1947.

Another Wrightian who left a number of important houses in San Diego was Sim Bruce Richards, who studied art at U.C. Berkeley, then apprenticed under Frank Lloyd Wright during the 1930s. Richards's houses, like Wright's, struck a balance between Modern (open plans and connections to the landscape through large and/or carefully placed windows) and mellow (lovingly crafted from cedar or redwood or adobe bricks,

often with big stone fireplaces), and were sensitively sited with the terrain.

But no accounting of Modern houses in San Diego would be complete without mention of Cliff May, the Los Angeles–based master of the California ranch-style house, who died in 1989. His low-slung houses of stucco, adobe, or wood were not sleek and modern in appearance, but they were the ultimate marriage of indoor and outdoor space. The houses, including several in San Diego County, featured L- or U-shaped arrangements of wings around terra-cotta-tiled courtyards with pools or fountains. Big sliding glass doors opened rooms to the courts. Trellises or deep eaves sheltered outdoor walkways that provided transitions from rooms to courtyards.

During the 1950s, several proteges of Ruocco began producing spare Modern houses on their own. One of the most prolific was Homer Delawie (still practicing), who graduated with a degree in architecture from Cal Poly San Luis Obispo in 1951, worked in Fresno for three years, and came to San Diego in 1954 to join Ruocco's office. They were partners from 1958 until 1961.

The house Delawie designed for himself in 1958 was a classic of Modern simplicity and ingenuity. It was a long, 17-foot-wide box sheathed with vertical cedar siding, set on wood posts and an L-shaped base of concrete block, with a carport tucked underneath.

Within this compact space, Delawie included a small interior courtyard garden that provided lush views to the dining area and master bedroom on either side, plus a tiny pocket garden in a back corner of the house defined by the walls of a children's bedroom and adjacent bath.

Delawie shared Ruocco's interest in European and California Modernism, ranging from Schindler to the Case Studies.

"I remember going out to see the Schindler buildings in La Jolla," says Delawie, "(El Pueblo Ribera, courtyard apartments of poured-in-place concrete); how very simple they were, how they tied into the coastal environment. I liked the work Mies van der Rohe was doing, the work Lloyd was doing, and Los Angeles Case Study architects such

"Box car" (1958) was a "calling card" house Delawie designed for himself as a young architect. Douglas M. Simmonds

Neutra's Oxley residence in La Jolla, completed in 1962, is an angular but low-key design for a moody coastal site.

as Craig Ellwood, Quincy Jones, Frederick Emmons, Whitney Smith, and Ed Killingsworth (a Los Angeles architect who designed San Diego's only Case Study houses, the early 1960s Triad development in La Jolla)."

Delawie's houses from the 1960s and 1970s, sheathed mostly in wood, had increasingly complex compositions that consisted of dynamic arrangements of cubic volumes. During the 1970s, Delawie began to vary his roof forms to add a new

energy to his designs. The house Delawie designed for himself in 1975, with its slanting shed roofs and weathered vertical wood siding, is reminiscent of Bay Area work from this period, including Charles Moore's condominiums at Sea Ranch up the California Coast from San Francisco.

Another San Diego Modernist was Paul McKim, who graduated from the University of Illinois with a degree in architecture in 1961 and opened his own San Diego office in 1963. McKim,

Los Angeles architect Ed Killingsworth designed the only Case Study houses (1960) in San Diego, the Triad Development in La Jolla. House B, seen from house A, has since been remodeled beyond recognition. Julius Shulman

Delawie's early 1960s Randolph house in Ocean Beach had an H-shaped plan with entrances from both alley and street, and was sited to preserve several old eucalyptus trees. Douglas M. Simmonds

Modernism meets wood siding and shed roofs in the house Delawie designed for himself in 1975. Michael Denny © 1993

McKim's house (1965, since remodeled) had tall volumes arranged around a central entry court. John Oldenkamp

who once had an office in the Ruocco-designed San Diego Design Center, names Los Angeles architect Richard Neutra as his main influence.

McKim's first house was a small place for himself completed in 1965, a simple but powerful design. The flat-roofed two-story house was arranged in an H-shape around two courtyard gardens, and the living room soared to double height. Tall vertical strip windows on the street-facing side of the house admitted natural light to the living room while retaining privacy. Walls around the back courtyard were floor-to-ceiling glass.

San Diego Modernists of the 1960s included Robert Jones, who went to U.S.C. during the 1950s and designed several Case Study–influenced houses in San Diego, along with Henry Hester and the partnership of Fred Liebhardt and Eugene Weston. Also, there was Hal Sadler, a U.S.C. graduate and former employee of Case Study architect Quincy Jones. In 1961, Sadler designed a stunningly transparent two-story house in Mission Beach, with huge walls of glass taking in waterfront views, and high ceilings tailored to its owner, a basketball player. Sadler has continued his commitment to spare Modern buildings, and still practices.

Some of these architects were well aware of the leading L.A. Modernists, not only through publications and Los Angeles houses, but through a

The case Study Houses influence is visible in Sadler's design of this house in Mission Beach (1962). George Lyons

By 1974, when Simpson and Gerber's Masek residence was completed, they were among several San Diego architects experimenting with new, dynamic geometries. Robert Ward

smattering of work in San Diego County. Harwell Hamilton Harris's Lek residence was completed in La Jolla in 1942, and Richard Neutra's Oxley house in La Jolla was finished in 1962.

B y the early 1970s, clean-lined Modernism was still a predominant style in San Diego, with lots of glass and open interior plans, but a new movement was beginning to erupt. Houses by Delawie, Sadler, and others, including Arthur Simpson and Joe Gerber grew more complex in their arrangements of planes and angles, becoming kinetic three-dimensional sculptures as opposed to the placid boxes of the 1950s and 1960s.

Some younger architects, including Rob Quigley and Ted Smith, started out designing relatively simple houses that obviously grew out of the earlier generation's work, but a new consciousness began to creep in. Quigley, Smith, Tom Grondona, and Randy Dalrymple, the core of an innovative late-1970s group in San Diego, had come of age during the rebellious 1960s. By the time they had their own architectural practices in the 1970s, challenging the status quo seemed like the natural thing to do.

Quigley, Smith, and Grondona rejected Modernism's cool efficiency and quest for viable universal theories and began to look in their own "backyard" for inspiration. They trolled the imme-

Quigley's Squire residence (1979) featured a concrete-block wall he imagined as a ruin found on site. Robert Ward

diate neighborhoods surrounding their San Diego projects for forms and materials that might be inventively incorporated into their designs. By the early 1980s, Quigley and Smith were using concrete block, asphalt shingle, and other basic materials. Along with the immediacy that came from their brand of contextualism, they were developing new, abstract ways of thinking about their buildings.

In designing the Squire residence in Del Mar (1978), Quigley imagined that a 1000-year-old wall had been unearthed on the site and incorporated into the new house. He fantasized that the Jaeger beach house (1984) in Del Mar was a cluster of pieces scattered by a tsunami. Not only did these story lines stimulate the architect, but he hoped they might provide clients with a sense of history in a region whose architectural history is thin.

Quigley's 1981 Sayer house in Mission Beach was a playful experiment in addressing beach culture. The house has industrial roll-up doors that merge interiors with a deck and the sights and

Industrial roll-up doors and rooftop hot tub were features that suited Quigley's Sayer beach house (1980) perfectly to its Mission Beach location. *Glenn M. Christiansen for* Sunset Magazine

Behind the mirrored "eraser" designed as part of a Case Study remodel (1980) of a 1950s rancher in Del Mar, Quigley placed a Queen Anne addition. *Marshall Harrington*

"Pig With A Purple Eye Patch" (1982), designed by Randy Dalrymple, was a cartoonish, sculptural house that reworked its neighborhood's bungalow roots.

Dalrymple's "Soldiers In Argyle" (1983) offended the Old Guard and inspired some among the younger set.

sounds of the nearby boardwalk. Several other decks become usable outdoor rooms, and a rooftop spa shaded by a steel-frame canvas awning gives the impression of a lifeguard tower.

Quigley selected green asphalt shingle and red detailing—sympathetic but contrasting colors—to accent the wood exterior, because he felt these colors might represent the "rhythms and chaotic vitality of the beachfront village."

In an even more experimental spirit, Quigley's "Case Study Remodel" of a Del Mar rancher in 1980 used a horizontal rooftop panel of mirrored glass to "erase" the Queen Anne/Shingle-style addition he added in back.

"The house was contemporary with Gehry's house in Santa Monica, a step away from the Modern movement," Quigley recalls. "At the time, I wasn't aware of his work, and it is interesting to

Platt's Patterson residence (1987) showed that younger San Diego architects had begun favorably reassessing the virtues of Gill's restrained approach. Phillip Scholz Rittermann

me that there was something in the air in southern California as a whole that found us trying some of these materials, in one way here, and in a more fine art way in Los Angeles. Gehry's much more sophisticated take was colored by his association with artists."

Houses designed by Quigley and Dalrymple ("Pig with A Purple Eye Patch," "Soldiers in Argyle") won design awards and drew national media attention to San Diego, but did not impress the local architectural Old Guard.

"Our residential architecture was much more organized," Sadler says, comparing his generation's work to the new stuff. "You zoned areas of living and sleeping, and used wings that would spread and open into special places, all tied together through the kitchen and the entry. It seemed to me that they (Quigley et al) lacked discipline or knowledge of structure and composition."

But in the 1990s, San Diego architecture, like some of the new architecture in Los Angeles and the San Francisco Bay Area, is coming full circle as architects including Quigley continue exploring new ideas while reconsidering older ones. There's

a growing respect, especially among the generation coming up behind Quigley, Grondona, and Smith, for the classic California Modernists of the 1920s through 1950s. Houses such as the Patterson residence, designed by the late San Diego architect Lee Platt, who passed away prematurely in 1990, show the direct influence of Gill.

Quigley, like Gill, is very much fascinated by the idea of southern California as a place of mythic possibilities, a contemporary Arcadia, a land of opportunity for great creativity.

"The older I get, the more profound Gill seems to me," Quigley says. "He was the first and maybe the only architect who synthesized the best tenets of the Modern movement with the history and culture of this particular region. To me, that was his great accomplishment. He took this idea that Kevin Starr articulates (in his book *Americans and the California Dream*) that southern California could blend Hispanic and Anglo cultures and become this place where freedoms and potentials exist that couldn't exist elsewhere."

In an essay published in the February 1991 issue of *Architecture California*, Quigley outlined his ideas on the quest for a regional architecture for southern California. One dilemma cited by Quigley applies to Gill and to San Diego architects and especially tract housing builders who for many years have leaned heavily on assorted Hispanic/Latin influences. With both tensions and opportunities along the San Diego/Mexico border at an all-time high, architects are increasingly aware of the need to consider the city's diverse heritage in their architecture.

"The best work of southern California architects has been tempered with concern for the more difficult aspects of regionalism," Quigley wrote. "From the seminal work of Gill and Schindler through a calculated Neutra and an intuitive Frank Gehry, their best work speaks to a spirit and identity that makes it uniquely southern Californian. In southern California the opportunity for a more authentic built environment may lie in the struggle to weave an architecture of cultural diversity and contradiction."

Nick Weiss grew up in England, fascinated by the sci-fi TV series "Dr. Who" and its time machine, the "Tardis."

Today Weiss and Linda Churchill are a husband-and-wife muralist team in San Diego, and the Tardis has been reincarnated as an entry tower that is the pivotal piece of a live-work studio addition to their tiny bungalow.

San Diego architect Jeanne McCallum designed the 700-square-foot addition, which steps down the sloping lot next to the original house. A curved bridge carries visitors from the street to the "Tardis" tower, an 8-foot-square semitransparent threshold to the exciting new space.

Beyond the tower, steel staircases connect three descending levels. The stairs drop next to a concrete block wall with translucent slot windows that filter light through strips of laminated glass. The first-level kitchen and dining room continue along the edge of the space, the second level is an office, and the lowest is the studio/living space, the heart of the house.

The west wall incorporates a "floating square" that becomes a canvas for Weiss and Churchill's murals, and they began with a rendition of Picasso's 1921 Cubist painting *Trés Musicians*. The artists also applied special finishes to the plywood floors.

A bridge crosses from street to entry tower, spanning Weiss and Churchill's outdoor work space. David Hewitt and Anne Garrison

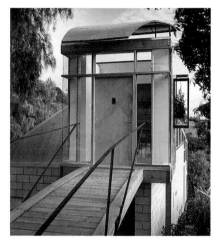

The transparent, transitional entry tower was inspired by the "Tardis," a time machine in an old British TV series. David Hewitt and Anne Garrison

A floating square is a canvas for Weiss and Churchill's murals, in this case a recreation of Picasso's 1921 Tres Musicians. *David Hewitt and Anne Garrison*

Three levels step down through the open space, with the artists' living room/studio on the bottom, open to the canyon through a sliding exposed wood-frame door. David Hewitt and Anne Garrison

Interior space soars to 20 feet beneath the open-beam ceiling. Small slot windows in the concrete block wall at left admit natural light. At right, the dining room thrusts into the space, offering a bird's eye view. David Hewitt and Anne Garrison

Decks extend two levels outdoors, beneath the shade of old pepper trees McCallum preserved as an integral part of her design. A cylindrical tower at the back of the house contains the new master bath above an open-air hot tub.

McCallum's addition is an assemblage of dynamic forms and spaces bound by the kind of tension one finds in good abstract paintings. There are few 90-degree angles. The new space broadens slightly from front to back, directing attention toward the lush canyon visible beyond an end wall of glass over exposed framing. The curved edge of the dining platform cantilevers daringly, and wood columns rise to support the 20-foot ceiling of tongue-and-groove fir.

In 1981, McCallum arrived in San Diego with an architecture degree from Auburn University, drawn by the city's exciting new architecture, and she has since come to admire Irving Gill's early Modern buildings there. Her design for Weiss and Churchill is free and energetic, but it also responds logically to a hillside site, the need for natural light and privacy, and the artists' casual, flowing lifestyle.

In San Diego County, many neighborhoods are dominated by Mediterranean-derived architecture or imported historic styles. Architect Ted Smith's blendo offers a more relevant approach. Smith draws elements from nearby buildings and collages them together in houses that look both fresh and hauntingly familiar.

Since the early eighties, Smith's designs have livened up Del Mar Terrace, a coastal enclave tucked among sandstone bluffs south of Del Mar. The neighborhood has houses in many sizes, shapes, and styles, from tiny clapboard bungalows to Modern boxes in wood and stucco to assorted revivals.

"You have architects dropping their latest vision of style onto a neighborhood," Smith

The house snuggles back into its sandstone bluff, a stack of cubes energized by roofs that fly off in different directions. David Hewitt and Anne Garrison

Blendo is the word Smith uses to describe how he blends materials drawn from the neighborhood, in this case concrete block, clapboards, stucco, and wood shingles. David Hewitt and Anne Garrison

A steel frame allows a spacious interior and huge aluminum-frame glass doors that open the central living space to the garden. A sliding barn door opens the studio to the garden, too. David Hewitt and Anne Garrison

Family living for the Carnicks is on one level, with kitchen, living, and dining rooms flowing together. David Hewitt and Anne Garrison

explains. "What you get is lots of buildings sitting next to each other that don't create any harmony or rhythm and that don't hang together. We take materials, dimensions, window types from adjacent buildings and put them into a collage that sort of unites them, so they're not sitting in conflict but in a composition together. You start to develop a feeling of continuity."

Smith's latest design in Del Mar Terrace was the result of a collaboration with his client, Debbie Carnick, an artist who turned up in Smith's design class at the New School of Architecture in San Diego. Smith designed the house with Carnick as his right-hand apprentice. He was responsible for big strokes such as siting, forms, structure, exterior materials, and the wide-open plan; she critiqued his design and attended to details, including cabinets and hardware.

The low-profile house, built with minimal grading, follows the lay of the land, snuggling into an existing notch in its sandstone bluff, preserving neighbors' ocean views.

A concrete block cube of a base contains the first-floor garage and kids' playroom, and the second-level the kids' rooms and a study. More expressive volumes are stacked above, jostled to capture views and natural light, crowned with slanting

Wood shingles used outside carry inside, blurring the distinction between indoor and outdoor space. A bridge connects the elevator (at right) with the master bedroom and library. David Hewitt and Anne Garrison

Instead of hiding concrete block, Smith elevates it to decorative status with a two-tone pattern. David Hewitt and Anne Garrison

shed roofs. Each volume is distinguished by its material: natural concrete block, yellow clapboards, white clapboards, gray stucco-steel-glass, green wood shingles.

The Carnicks have two sons, one of whom is confined to a wheelchair, and they wanted a house with main living spaces on one level. They ended up with four levels, but the living and dining rooms and kitchen inhabit the open third floor. A steel-cage elevator rises through the open core of the house.

Steel framing allowed open interiors and broad expanses of glass. Eight-foot-high aluminum-frame sliding doors and a concrete floor that continues on a single plane into the garden enhance the continuum of space from indoors and out, in classic California Modern tradition dating back to R. M. Schindler's 1922 house in Hollywood.

Carnick designed maple and cherry kitchen cabinets, and Smith specified corrugated plastic for closet doors, waxed concrete floors, and vinyl floor tiles laid in colorful checkerboards.

"I like to use simple materials like concrete block and aluminum windows and let them show, an old Modernist aesthetic that saves money," Smith says. "But it takes little touches like the concrete block *coins* in the playroom to make it come across. I don't believe in the architect as complete craftsman. We're more in tune with artistic aspirations."

A rchitect Randy Dalrymple's house in upscale old Mission Hills is an aggressive experiment in breaking down barriers between indoors and out, and in family living without the separation of conventional walls.

Since the early eighties, Dalrymple has been responsible for some of San Diego's most inventive homes, including a pair of cartoonish places that earned the nicknames "Soldiers in Argyle" and "Pig with Purple Eye Patch."

But these were largely graphic exercises, exterior treatments that livened up existing homes. "Home Sweet Home," the place Dalrymple designed for himself, his wife, and their teenage daughter, carries his imagination into three dimensions.

The exterior is a dynamic collage of elements borrowed from nearby houses: clapboard siding, gabled roofs, a white picket fence, combined with oversized windows that flap open, inviting in coastal breezes and natural light. Living here is like camping out. A skylight over the dining room slides open to the sky, a giant "ventilator" window drops away from the living room's front wall, and someday, Dalrymple hopes to rig his bed to slide out under the stars.

"Home Sweet Home" presents a friendly "face" with a "mouth" that opens the living room wide to warm weather.
David Hewitt and Anne Garrison

A flying bridge crosses from top-floor front door to living room. David Hewitt and Anne Garrison

A sliding skylight opens the dining room to the sky. Dalrymple eliminated corners, rejecting the conventional definition of "room."
David Hewitt and Anne Garrison

An initial visit can cause giddy sensations. Entry stairs climb up across the front of the house behind the diagonal slash of picket fencing to a second-floor corner entry, and a wooden bridge connects the threshold with the living room. Clapboard siding carries inside along some walls, blurring the distinction between indoors and out.

Dalrymple has blown apart the traditional house and reassembled it anew. Rooms seem suspended in space, without conventional interior walls connecting them to the shell. Traditional rooms—kitchen, dining, study, bedrooms, baths—are all here, but in fresh incarnations. Without doors or conventional walls lending traditional privacy, the interior dictates an uninhibited mode of living that might shock traditionalists.

The plan consists of several squares, stacked and colliding, joined at corners. Outer walls align with the rectangular lot, but most inner walls cut energizing diagonals.

Dalrymple wanted his daughter to feel the house was equally hers, so he gave her the biggest bedroom. It lives up to every kid's fantasy of a secluded fortress away from adults, tucked in a lower corner of the house, equipped with private patio and a bed that cantilevers into the double-height space from atop one wall. The master

From the back, the house is a transparent collage animated by flaps and sliding panels. The master bedroom is behind a pop-out sliding door at lower left, the living room is beyond big windows at right. David Hewitt and Anne Garrison

Dalrymple's house is an experimental work-in-progress, with spaces that flow freely together related intimately to the outdoors. David Hewitt and Anne Garrison

bedroom is on the second level, and living and dining rooms and a small study occupy the third floor, where they take advantage of the height to gain sweeping views.

Doing dishes at the sink in the corner of the kitchen, with two big windows flapped open, the Dalrymples look out at the green of a nearby nursery and the distant blue strip of ocean. A giant chalkboard serves as a divider between the kitchen and living room. Guests contribute art or words, such as one story that stayed there for weeks and seemed to capture the fastastic spirit of Home Sweet Home. It began:

"If all goes as planned on Mar. 30, Queen Beatrix will glide past a huge field of sunflowers on the museum plein outside the Rijksmuseum . . ."

Like the changing chalkboard displays, Dalrymple sees his house as a work in progress.

It still has many unfinished details, but this building is not about craftsmanship. Dalrymple's San Diego experiment in spatial organization and indoor/outdoor living belongs to a southern California continuum of innovators that began with R. M. Schindler and Irving Gill.

R N P

A sleek new house rises phoenixlike from the ashes of its predecessor after a devastating canyon fire. For San Diego architects Ralph Roesling and Kotaro Nakamura, history is a source of inspiration that manifests in subtle ways.

Poised at the edge of a finger canyon, the replacement house they designed for Bob and Bunnye Meisel is a stripped abstraction of the vanquished bungalow. A gabled form hovers like a ghostly reincarnation of the original house between two flat-roofed cubes. The entry, with its concrete column, stainless-steel-covered door, and sparse, scrubby landscaping, is a pale memory of deep vine-covered bungalow porches.

"The expression is very harsh and cold and inhumane, and that's exactly what I was looking for," says Nakamura. Bunnye Meisel, an interior designer who worked closely with the architects, agreed.

"They consider the life inside to be like painting or art," Nakamura says. "The house is treated like a museum. Say you are sitting on the couch, drinking coffee. That activity is art. The person becomes the artwork in the museum."

Beneath the gabled roof, a double-height, gallery-like central living space is furnished with pieces designed by Bunnye. A serpentine concrete block wall slithers along one side like a snake headed toward the dry canyon.

The wall separates this formal area from the kitchen/dining room, where the Meisels often take a dip in a hot tub with a dramatic view of Mission Valley and a freeway interchange that dances with car headlights at night. On the other side of the central space are the first-floor master bed-

Cool, minimal materials such as gray stone pavers, concrete columns, and a stainless-steel-skinned front door make the house a neutral container for art and life within. Ed Gohlich

San Diego artist Steven Lombardi's stainless-steel clock rests at the juncture of crisscrossing stairs that lead up to two offices. Glenn Cormier

Bob's office looks down on the living room, with custom furniture designed by Bunnye. Stainless-steel detailing includes cove base moldings. Glenn Cormier

The central living space, with its hard edges and subdued colors, is intended as a gallery-like place animated by art and people. Concrete block wall separates this formal core from the kitchen/dining area behind it. Glenn Cormier

A hot tub set in the dining room looks down a canyon toward a busy freeway intersection crossed at night by a steady stream of car headlights. Glenn Cormier

A gabled form rises phoenixlike, symbolizing how this new, contemporary place rose from the ashes of its traditional predecessor. A curved concrete block wall echoes the shape of the canyon bowl behind the house. Ed Gohlich

room and second-level offices. Each office has its own stairs, and the offices are not connected on the second level, emphasizing each as a private domain.

Materials maintain a cool aesthetic: smooth-troweled stucco, crisp, smooth plaster walls, concrete block, stainless-steel railings, concrete steps, gray commercial carpeting, bleached white oak flooring, charcoal-gray stone pavers.

For Roesling and Nakamura, partners since 1983, the Meisel residence was another step in a process of paring their architecture to essentials.

"I'm really taken with the Los Angeles Case Study houses," Roesling says. "They were intelligent, simple responses to the landscape and climate. I'm also influenced by Schindler's honesty with materials, expressing things so clearly that it's almost resounding. This house is so smooth it reflects light like houses in Greece and Portugal, popping out from the landscape like a jewel."

Christmas season, and red and green smoke streams from twin towers atop the Beaumont Building. San Diego architect Rob Wellington Quigley and his family have invited friends to celebrate the holidays at their rooftop aerie, and guests are greeted by a roaring fire in the circular courtyard's fireplace.

Quigley lives and works in this five-story building he designed when he decided to move to the city's revitalizing core. His was one of the first new buildings granted legitimate live/work status so tenants can use their spaces as homes, offices, studios, or some combination.

Urban planners believe such mixed use can help crowded, smoggy places like southern California remain livable by keeping people out of their cars and recharging downtowns with twenty-four-hour-a-day populations. Quigley makes the most of the efficient setup. He climbs a flight of stairs to join his wife and young daughter for lunch, or shuffles down to his drafting board in the middle of the night when brainstorms hit.

Rooms of Quigley's compact penthouse are strung around the courtyard in a continuous arc. The court is an outdoor living room that puts a new urban spin on notions of casual indoor/outdoor living that date back to the houses of

At night, Quigley's building is a shadowy, amorphous abstraction of forms and materials found nearby. David Hewitt and Anne Garrison

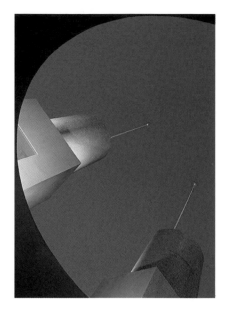

The twin towers of Quigley's five-story mixed-use building in downtown San Diego rise above the courtyard rim atop his rooftop aerie. Rob Quigley

early California Modernists, including R. M. Schindler.

The building abstracts and collages forms and materials found in the area. Twin towers pay homage to many San Diego towers, including a pair on a nearby church. Commercial aluminum-sash windows open a dialogue with nearby office buildings, but other elements add residential scale and character, including an arch that embraces both auto and pedestrian entries, colorful ceramic-tile decoration, a tiny pocket balcony that looks down on the sidewalk, and flowering vines that climb walls or drape down from above.

Neither office nor condo, Quigley's building is provocative, amorphous, difficult to "read."

"I didn't want it to look like an apartment building or offices," he says. "The image is intentionally ambiguous, and that's the quality most people react to, sometimes positively, sometimes negatively."

Oversize nonfunctional stairs climb a front corner of the building, inviting viewers to participate in this mysterious composition. Pyramidal skylights above Quigley's fourth-floor drafting room pop into the fifth-floor courtyard as sculptural objects, and gray stucco exterior walls

Three-panel aluminum-sash glass doors flank pyramidal skylights, opening the living room wide to the central court. Skylights spill natural light into Quigley's office below. Rob Quigley

Main living areas are strung in an arc around the central court: kitchen (at far end), dining room (back corner), and living room. Tiles of recycled tire rubber cover the floor. Rob Quigley

Gray stucco takes on a golden glow at sunset, behind translucent pyramidal skylight. Rob Quigley

make a shadowy, reclusive impression.

"I liked the idea of creating a building that absorbs light instead of reflecting it," Quigley says. "It's hard to photograph. It likes to disappear from film."

To reach Quigley's "front door," you ride an elevator with rusted steel doors, departing from a lobby with walls of concrete block and poured-in-place concrete. Recessed into the elevator's teak walls are display boxes containing toy animals, trees, buildings, and odd pieces of hardware. Passengers are free to alter these dioramas.

Up top, you step onto a sunny south-facing public terrace intended for all building tenants, then through a modest entry into Quigley's private courtyard. Multi-panel doors open rooms wide to the court, and tiles of recycled tire rubber cover outdoor and indoor floors, enhancing the continuous flow of space. The courtyard is a cloistered, private escape from the encroaching city, the hub amid a ring of living spaces. Quigley's kitchen gets the best of both worlds, with teak-frame glass doors opening one corner to the

court and big south- and west-facing windows taking in urban views: San Diego Bay, the Art Deco–era County Administration Center a few blocks to the west, and a forest of downtown high-rises to the south.

Looking up from the oculus of the courtyard as the party winds down with an impromptu jazz jam, you see spotlighted silhouettes of twin towers against the stars as whispers of sax and guitar float out over the city.

San Diego architect Wallace Cunningham compares the house to a DNA molecule, with contrasting elements bound together by rhythmic, organic logic.

Crisp, rectilinear forms in monochromatic stucco, concrete, and plaster respond to a narrow site in oceanfront La Jolla, but the formal design also grew out of client Bennet Greenwald's ties to legendary architect Ludwig Mies van der Rohe. Greenwald's father built several Mies-designed high-rises along Chicago's famous Lakeshore Drive.

Cunningham, who studied architecture at Frank Lloyd Wright's Taliesin, is known for wildly individualistic homes that spread organic curves and angles across expansive sites, but an urban location provoked a tighter design that Cunningham says was his first to make extensive use of 90-degree angles.

"Cityhouse," as owner Judy Kennedy calls this place, con-

Louvered forms admit light but maintain privacy. Daylight washes edges of interior walls and ceilings, admitted by narrow horizontal clerestories. David Hewitt and Anne Garrison

A transparent glass entry offers an oblique view of the central courtyard. Sunlight stripes walls and concrete floor, admitted by narrow skylights. David Hewitt and Anne Garrison

An island in this serious kitchen stretches like the deck of an aircraft carrier. The guest pavilion is visible in back. David Hewitt and Anne Garrison

Vertical strip windows divide walls into individual art-display panels. David Hewitt and Anne Garrison

sists of three pieces in a *U* around a central courtyard, with two pieces along one edge of the property cupping a longer center section along the opposite edge. The living room is in the front portion, bedrooms and kitchen in the center, and guest quarters in the rear. Diagonal paths between pieces add a perspective of distance within the tight property.

For privacy, the house is set back from the street and elevated above the garage. A choreographed entry sequence reveals it: through a steel gate, up stairs that rise in front of the living room, to an ocean-view terrace. Glimpses of garden, kitchen, and sun-dappled interiors pull vistors through the glass entry and compact foyer to the expansive kitchen. Space explodes

vertically and horizontally, and a 17-foot-tall bank of glass looks out on designer Takendo Arii's landscape.

Daylight spills into the house through horizontal strips of glass set between the stepped, louverlike roof forms, and upper-level rooms are open to the kitchen below, sharing their daylight. Vertical strip windows divide walls into 5-foot panels

A central staircase captures the house's spare, sculptural essence, alive with the play of daylight from several directions. David Hewitt and Anne Garrison

Sensuous curves in Takendo Arii's landscape soften the house's hard edges. David Hewitt and Anne Garrison

for displaying paintings, and the strips admit daylight while retaining privacy from neighbors only 8 feet away.

"Some days the house is full of light," Kennedy says. "On summer days it looks cobalt blue, like the ocean, then changes to lavender as the sun sets. My favorite time is early morning or late afternoon in a winter rain. There's so much glass, I'm constantly aware of the weather changing, and I almost feel like I'm in a ship at sea."

P roblem sites can provoke wildly creative solutions. This steep, 16-by-75 site presented its share of headaches, but it also came with big views of downtown San Diego and the bayfront. San Diego architect Brad Burke of Studio E Architects snapped it up at a good price and let the location inspire a house for himself and his young family.

The narrow lot dictated a basic box to produce maximum living space, but Burke and fellow designer Eric Naslund triangulated their way out of the box with a diagonal wall of wood and glass that slashes across the third and fourth floors, with windows aimed at the best views. The wall generates intriguing interior spaces before it juts outside to culminate in a wood-frame prow that points toward San Diego Bay.

Concrete block, stucco, wood, and steel, all common local materials, come together in straightforward but inventive ways. The block base serves as ballast for light off-white stucco walls. Exposed steel beams, emphasized with purple paint, become both structure and decoration. Wood windows and other wood details, including mahogany veneer plywood panels used to sheath a portion of the exterior, add a warmth and softness that contrast with adjacent hard angles and stark sur-

faces. A cap of deep green stucco and a barrel-vaulted metal roof hold this buoyant ship to earth.

The steep lot dictated a plan that climbs the hillside, which means plenty of exercise for the Burkes, but also exciting interior volumes. From the ground-level garage, the house steps up by half levels—front-back, front-back—to a home studio, family room, music room, living/ kitchen/dining area, powder room, master bedroom, and kids' room.

Burke grew up in Los Angeles beach communities and takes great interest in the evolution of southern California architecture. He feels this house, while not a direct descendant of homes designed by R. M. Schindler in Los Angeles or Irving Gill in Los Angeles and San Diego, is faithful to the architectural heritage of the region.

Like Schindler, Burke orchestrated simple geometric forms into a rhythmic, dynamic whole. Like Gill, he used smooth stucco walls with windows slightly inset to create subtle shadow lines. And like many southern California architects before him, Burke employed floor-to-ceiling glass and big custom glass doors to capture natural light, views, and fresh air.

Burke was pleased by the way his roots in southern Cali-

Burke's house steps up its steep lot, preserving views for neighbors, creating decks that serve as the only usable outdoor spaces. David Hewitt and Anne Garrison

Entry is up the left side, behind a mahogany plywood pop-out. The wood frame points toward San Diego Bay like the prow of a ship. David Hewitt and Anne Garrison

fornia found expression in this house.

"Living with the beach every day, outdoors, with the sunshine and breezes, has definitely been

Pivoting wood doors open the living room to the deck and spectacular views of Lindbergh Field (San Diego's airport) and San Diego Bay. David Hewitt and Anne Garrison

a big influence," he says. "That's why this house has so much light and operable windows. Architects who are tied into particular styles are avoiding a discussion of regionalism because it will force them to address issues that are more relevant than what a building looks like."

The view from master bedroom shows how Burke oriented the diagonal side wall toward downtown San Diego. David Hewitt and Anne Garrison

Los Angeles is internationally known as the birthplace of the California bungalow, but other West Coast cities including San Diego received their share of these practical, modest cottages during the early years of this century. Del Mar architect John Nalevanko combined rustic bungalow elements with dashes of East Coast "salt box" and contemporary spice to transform this ocean-view home in Del Mar.

Locals in this ocean-side village are protective of traditions, and Nalevanko's remodel responds to the woodsy design vernacular and to its natural setting. Cedar shingles and aqua-green trim empathize with nearby ocean, eucalyptus, and Torrey pines, and a gray stucco base roots the house to earth like the stone and brick bases used by California bungalow pioneers Greene and Greene in Los Angeles.

Nalevanko used banks of glass block in the south front wall to admit natural light to the kitchen and living room while maintaining privacy, and added awnings that pop out to protect interiors from high hot summer sun. He raised a soaring tent-like roof over the central living space that slopes like the roof on a salt box, supported it with a treelike Doric column, and added a rear window wall with sweeping whitewater views.

Kitchen, dining, and living rooms flow together in the compact central space, made to seem expansive by the open plan, 16-foot cedar ceilings, and an easily accessible terrace.

Interiors were lovingly de-

Narrow space between the street and house is made dramatic by processional entry. Steel-and-wood awnings shade south-facing windows. Arched forms become a unifying design theme. Joan Vanderschuit

Sleek white kitchen cabinets just inside the entry were designed by Nalevanko. Joan Vanderschuit

Treelike Douglas fir column and rafters support cedar ceiling in the living room. The column is actually a decorative sleeve that contains a 6-by-6-inch bearing column. Joan Vanderschuit

tailed. Douglas fir beams and rafters were mortised and tenoned together like fine furniture, and walls are smooth plaster with rounded corners.

Nalevanko studied architecture at Cal Poly Pomona and apprenticed with San Diego architects Tucker Sadler & Bennett, seasoned, committed Modernists. Later, he worked for San Diego architect Ted Smith, who conceived a blendo approach to contextualism that involves collaging forms and materials found on adjacent buildings.

On his own since 1980, Nalevanko has evolved his own way of tailoring houses such as the Nugents' to their locales. "Component architecture," according to Nalevanko, is both a means of defining a project up front, and a method for developing a design.

"Typically, architects prioritize the elements that shape a design," he says. "Sometimes, important considerations such as energy conservation, durability, and how the furniture will fit in a room lose out to more tangible concerns such as style and materials. I look at these items in a linear, harmonious way and try to balance them in each design."

Nalevanko's "component architecture" also refers to the physical components of a building.

"We look at the various pieces, from whole rooms to individual windows, and articulate and emphasize each piece within a unified whole. San Diego is stylistically and culturally chaotic, and our component method is adaptable to different neighborhoods. It's a fluid, flexible approach to designing buildings that succeed on many levels."

As the sun sets over the ocean west of Del Mar, surfers slice across waves and the blaring horn of an Amtrak train echoes up from the Del Mar station. The Nugent house is pleasingly fresh but also as comforting as these familiar daily rituals.

Nalevanko-designed "Nollo" chairs rest on an ocean-view deck and terrace behind panoramic living room windows. Joan Vanderschuit

San Diego architect Eric Naslund's house wraps around an old mock orange tree in a courtyard, with decks and windows affording intimate views of its dark, gnarled branches. The house strikes a pleasing balance between nature and structure.

Naslund and John Sheehan at Studio E Architects began the design for a speculative developer, but as the house came to life

Highly visible second-floor dining and living rooms make friendly gestures to the neighborhood. David Hewitt and Anne Garrison

A galvanized steel wall reflects the dining room table. Playing with perceptions of indoors and out, Naslund used an aluminum exterior window as a food pass-through from the kitchen. David Hewitt and Anne Garrison

Floors are waxed particleboard with inlaid strips of pine. The light monitor pops up over the kitchen to bring in extra daylight. Counters are blue-green plastic laminate, cabinets are painted fiberboard. David Hewitt and Anne Garrison

on the drafting board, with inviting outdoor spaces and rooms tucked cozily among the upper branches of the tree, Naslund and his wife fell in love with the place. So they bought the property and built the house for themselves.

In this Golden Hill neighborhood just east of downtown San Diego, there are buildings from every decade beginning with the 1890s. Naslund's house borrows vertical thrust from neighboring Victorians and

boxy forms from "dingbat" fifties stucco apartment buildings.

The 2200-square-foot house consists of vertical putty-colored stucco boxes connected by a yellow clapboard entry/stair tower, with rooms arranged so that those most frequently used get the best views. Kids' bedrooms and the garage are on the first floor, with the kitchen/dining space and living room on the second, and the master suite on the third. A quirky "light moni-

tor" that vaguely resembles a railroad car pops up over the kitchen to bring in natural light.

Since the house is only one room deep, each room gets excellent cross ventilation and natural light from several directions. A rooftop deck with a fireplace takes advantage of spectacular downtown and San Diego Bay views, while the second-level wood deck off the kitchen is a logical extension of indoor living space. Abundant, carefully placed windows offer

Stucco and clapboard volumes cluster in a U around an old mock orange tree visible from every room. David Hewitt and Anne Garrison

A deck extends kitchen space into the garden, beneath the gnarled limbs of the old mock orange tree. David Hewitt and Anne Garrison

different perspectives on the old mock orange, a mature, friendly presence felt in most every room.

Although the neighborhood is on the upswing, it is still known for its high crime rate, but Naslund relied more on good planning than traditional security to make his home feel safe. A low gated wall across the front of the property is an extension of his neighbor's wall, a sign that Naslund's house is a part of the neighborhood fabric, not an isolated interloper. Upper-level living and dining rooms are plainly visible from the street, a friendly gesture to neighbors, and a small balcony pops out from the living room in another warm salute.

Subtle tweaks to the home's basic geometry achieve dramatic results and hint at tension in the changing, ethnically diverse community. The south stucco volume turns away from its north sister slightly to align windows with views through a gap between neighboring buildings, and to lend an expansive feeling to the compact courtyard, which widens from front to back.

Interior circulation is hall-less, with stairs climbing through the entry tower, and an outdoor bridge connects the master suite to the rooftop deck, with its widow walk around the railroad-car light monitor.

Naslund laid floors, installed railings, and handled numerous other finish details, keeping construction cost to a rock-bottom $68 per square foot, proving that low budgets don't have to mean low art.

Spare stucco volumes around a courtyard are one sign that Naslund, who earned his architecture degree from Cal Poly San Luis Obispo, admires early twentieth-century San Diego architect Irving Gill, but he is also in tune with the far-out Los Angeles houses of the 1980s.

"Eric Moss's Petal House is all about the hot tub on the roof, a classic California idea," says Naslund of the place Moss completed in 1982. "Architects on the East Coast love to hate it, but they love to love it too, because they could never do that back east. In California, you don't have to worry about extreme winter weather and as a consequence, the building is much lighter, more ephemeral.

"In terms of regional architecture in San Diego, it primarily has to do with how you take advantage of the climate. A real southern California house does that in kind of an effortless way, with rooms spilling out onto decks, interior space flowing to the outside, with a casual *joie de vivre* that just happens because it's possible and easy to do."

Towers are common in San Diego, ranging from architect Bertram Goodhue's ornate circa-1915 Spanish Colonial spire in Balboa Park to the cylindrical cupolas of several Queen Anne Victorians. Architects Rene Davids and Christine Killory took the tower to a new level of abstraction, jolting their sleepy San Diego neighborhood wide awake with this library addition to their 1930s stucco bungalow.

Davids and Killory have a love/hate thing going with Southern California, where movies, television, and assorted beach phenomena long ago replaced books as the most significant cultural forces. Educated in England, they came to San Diego in 1987 because it was a place where young, progressive architects could make a mark in a rapidly growing city.

Dedicated to architecture as an intellectual pursuit that requires constant study, the architects played up their new

The library tower gave a radical facelift to Davids and Killory's traditional stucco bungalow. Joan Vanderschuit

A ladder leads from the second level of the library to rooftop deck. Joan Vanderschuit

Black marble covers the observatory cube, a place for reading, writing letters, watching cars, and people. Joan Vanderschuit

library as a highly visible icon for literacy along their conservative, palm-lined street.

In San Diego, old Spanish-flavored bungalows, like theirs was before its facelift, are often remodeled in pseudo-Mediterranean styles intended to blend in. Often, however, these makeovers are poorly proportioned and suffer from a lack of proper detailing.

Davids and Killory opted for a radical departure, altering their home's identity with a new stucco- and marble-clad tower and a salmon-colored front wall that encloses the original porch and camouflages the old house. Rectilinear forms generate a tension reminiscent of abstract expressionist paintings by Mondrian or Kandinsky.

The tower is a two-story box, augmented by cantilevered shading devices, a projecting second-level reading room, and a diagonal stair that connects the second story with a rooftop observatory. Rows of small, rectangular openings punch through the sides of the tower, admitting natural light, adding fine-grained scale, helping to organize the exterior. A vertical slit window and skylight bisect the top of the tower, aligning with the interior stairs, providing light that draws visitors up through the tower.

Inside, the architects selected solid, basic materials and handled them with care. Reading room walls are paneled with basswood, neatly attached with countersunk screws, the holes covered with plugs of exotic African padouk wood. A single round steel column at the center of the tower is painted red, which adds a splash of color and accentuates its importance as a

Staggered steel steps rise through the tower's core to a second-level catwalk and the observatory cube. Tiny slot windows admit daylight and become a rhythmic decorative element on the exterior. *Joan Vanderschuit*

The kitchen has Corian counters and bird's eye maple cabinets. Joan Vanderschuit

A marble-clad tower-top perch offers a panoramic view that takes in other area towers. A strip skylight provides extra daylight to the library. Joan Vanderschuit

structural element. Steel steps rise from the library to the tower-top reading room.

Besides the new library, the other major change was a sleek makeover of the tiny original kitchen, with gray Corian counters, bird's-eye maple cabinets, and black appliances. The compact but efficient layout includes a dining nook for two and a small desk for making notes while talking on the phone.

Davids and Killory's architecture is visually stunning, but the exteriors of the place they call "Observatory House" are not random shock-value forms. Instead, they are logical expressions of interior function: the need for light and privacy, ample book storage, and the architects' desire for a secluded bird's-nest perch of a reading room that captures sweeping views of the city.

With this dynamic addition, Davids and Killory prove that you don't have to go on a nostalgia trip to successfully remodel a vintage home. They came to southern California because they admire its free-spirited new architecture. They are finding new ways to address regional conditions without resorting to timeworn clichés.

Somewhere in San Diego, a gentle summer day, the area is steep, the natural vegetation is carefully moving in the light wind, a cicada can be heard in the not so far distance. Appearing a bit lost, two gentlemen stand in the Julyish dust, and while one is wiping some sweat from his forehead, the other suddenly steps forward in an episode of unexpected energy, pointing uphill, and full excitement turns his head back to his companion.

STEVEN SPIELBERG (SS): Look George! There it is! Just like Dirk Sutro said, the site for a remake of "The Hidden Fortress."[1] What do you think?

GEORGE LUCAS (GL): Looks like just another European castle ruin to me, Steven, only you won't be able to blow the whole thing up in the final scene. The way this thing is built, all that concrete, and that rebar looks thicker than Arnold Schwarzenegger's arm. It will take more than a light saber to cut through that.

SS: Actually, I prefer this feeling of permanence and endurance, and I think you are just in a bad mood because it is so far away from Hollywood.

"That must be it, the Hidden Fortress."
G-shot ©

"This thing is real," he said with a tone of surprise, "it is not a set." G-shot ©

Besides, you have already done your "Hidden Fortress" remake.[2] I mine want to be more authentic.

GL: What do you mean?

SS: Don't get me wrong, I really liked yours. It's just that I would like the symbols to be much less obvious in my version. I want the story to be felt more through the imagination than through the senses, with Technicolor, wide screen and Surround Sound.

GL: I guess you are right. If you want to retain the mystery, you cannot do all those noisy and high colored special effects. Besides, everybody uses that stuff in their work now, and it gets hard to tell if there is any art left under all the pizazz.

SS: Exactly, come over here and stand more in the middle of it.

GL: You know, it takes awhile to notice, but there are more little details here than on our sound stages. And then there is this strange feeling of mystery.

SS: I feel it too, and I wonder what it is? Different for sure, but it seems it would help a

[1] "The Hidden Fortress." Directed by Akira Kurosawa, starring Toshiro Mifune and Minoru Chiaki, 1958, 126 minutes.

[2] "Star Wars." Directed by George Lucas, staring Mark Hamill, Harrison Ford, Carrie Fisher, and Alec Guinness, 1977, 121 minutes.

"Now is that a ruin, or is it not completed yet?" Steven was wondering, but George could not say for sure either. G-shot ©

"Careful George, they may still live here." G-shot ©

And turning to his companion he asked: "How do you tell the difference between the entrance and the exit of the underworld?" G-shot ©

"Which ever way you choose, you won't know what you will find." G-shot ©

"Slow down Steven, I can't climb so fast. Besides, these big drop-offs make me nervous." G-shot ©

project where the emphasis is on the individual fantasy rather than on prefabricated solutions.

GL: Part of it might be that wherever you look or step, you cannot quite predict what you will see or come upon.

SS: You are right, and something else just happened.

GL: What ?

SS: I can no longer tell whether this place is not yet finished, or whether it is far past its completion and has reached the stage of being a ruin.

GL: It probably does not matter, since this way it will always be in its prime state of existence.

SS: Hey, do you think I can get Stephen Hawking to do a guest appearance and explain why time seems to stand still on this site?

GL: If he's not afraid to come up that precarious driveway. But in any case, you will not have to worry about which is better: fading into black or fading into white. The emotion of this place is quite beyond the usual and simple 'the good guys versus the bad guys' plot."

SS: Maybe I should also do a remake of "Journey to the Center of the Earth"[3] or "Orpheus."[4] It feels like this building would hold hidden somewhere that special entrance.

[3] "Journey to the Center of the Earth." Directed by Henry Levin, starring James Mason, Pat Boone, and Arlene Dahl, 1959, 132 minutes.

[4] "Orpheus," directed by Jean Cocteau, starring Jean Marais and Maria Casares, 1949, 86 minutes.

GL: May the Force be with you on all these projects.

SS: When you say that, while we are standing here, I realize that the symbol of the "Force" means to just be one-self, and original. And without fear about possibly not belonging to the current trend or mainstream, for which the "Evil Empire" is the symbol you have used.

GL: Then maybe you should forget about doing re-makes and let your film be an original piece of art, sitting in a category all its own.

SS: So what is the difference between a re-make and an original that has received stimulation from some already existing ideas?

GL: It feels different. A simple re-make just never has a force of its own.

And their minds began to wander towards unusual places, in a galaxy far, far away. G-shot ©

"Is that buttress moving, George?" G-shot ©

"The purpose, the purpose? I can't quite understand the purpose." G-shot ©

"If you build a tower, she will come." G-shot ©

"Where is the tower, George?" G-shot ©

"Orpheus, is that you?" G-shot ©

"What ever you do," Orpheus said, "do not look back!" G-shot ©

INDEX